TROUT OF THE THAMES

A Superbly Grown Large Young Trout

TROUT OF THE THAMES

By

A. EDWARD HOBBS,
M.Inst., R.A.

[1947]

HERBERT JENKINS LIMITED
3 DUKE OF YORK STREET
ST. JAMES'S LONDON S.W.1

A
HERBERT
JENKINS
BOOK

First printing

Printed in Great Britain by Wyman & Sons Ltd., London, Reading and Fakenham

My thanks are heartily given to Mr. R. L. Marston, Editor of *The Fishing Gazette*, for his permission to re-use the basic portion of the following pages.

A. E. H.

FOREWORD

TROUT OF THE THAMES

" BEYOND any doubt," wrote Patrick R. Chalmers in " At the Tail of the Weir," " if you, or your boatman, can mount a dead bleak on a Thames flight so that it will spin like a flash of diamonds, there is no bait to approach it. I can tell you how to mount it, of course, but I cannot tell you how to make it spin, for I have not the magic of the finger tips. Which is, to-day, almost a lost magic and only known to one amateur of Thames and one of the few remaining professionals. And here, before I talk further of Thames trout fishing, I am going to quote Mr. Sheringham, who has written " There is only one man alive who has any business to mention a Thames trout in print—and he is Mr. A. E. Hobbs ! The above in self-extenuation."

We feel highly privileged and we are sure a great many of our readers will be delighted to hear that Mr. A. Edward Hobbs has chosen the pages of *The Fishing Gazette* to fulfil the duty which Mr. Sheringham's words imposed upon him. We leave our readers to the pleasant task of reading Mr. Hobbs's record of his long experience of Thames trout fishing, a record of remarkable catches and thrilling stories of big fish caught and of bigger fish which lived to fight another day.

R. L. M.

CONTENTS

ILLUSTRATIONS

AUTHOR'S PREFACE

IT being difficult to give an entirely satisfactory reason, it becomes necessary to offer a reasonably good excuse for adding even this small volume to the existing plethora of literature dealing with the Thames, its fish, fishing, and other amenities.

Without a tinge of shame I pass the blame—if blame it be—to a considerable number of my angling friends who have from time to time insisted that it is my duty to place on record at least some of the happenings which have come my way in the course of a very long experience of our grand old river and its trout.

Of the latter I have made a most interesting study from its egg to the appearance of one of its kind as an outstanding specimen mounted in a museum case, and can only hope that this small book will prove of interest to readers.

As will be found, it does not profess to teach a body how to fish ; other works can do that quite well, but as I am not acquainted with any other volume dealing exclusively with " Trout of the Thames " I feel that its appearance may be not altogether untimely.

A. E. H.

TROUT OF THE THAMES

CHAPTER I

A TROUT-FISHER IS BORN

THAMES Trouting is a kind of high fever—that is to say to the enthusiast—and a regularly recurring fever year after year at that. It does not readily respond to treatment, and the only certain and complete cure is change of venue of the patient—this word may be used in more than one sense—from Thames to Styx.

I caught my first dose of the said fever by way of my father who was very partial to a nicely-cooked perch of his own catching, and a good judge too, many will say.

One of his favourite perch swims was above the old weir at Marsh where one could, in those days of long ago, frequently see many very fine perch nosing for shrimps in the moss and weed which grew liberally on the old piles and paddles.

High times with me were those when I was allowed, in my school holidays, to accompany him on his occasional evening expeditions to catch a fry, and on one such occasion my father was held up by a friend whom he had not seen for many years, and a long exchange of experiences was inevitable.

After a few minutes of their conversation had passed I was allowed to take over the precious rod and tackle, the hook of which was baited with a brandling, of which delectable worm, my father could always gather a supply from a friend's old manure pit.

Becoming restless at not having a bite in the most favoured perch corner, I dared to divert the tackle to a little streamy run toward the paddles, and soon was thrilled to see the float disappear with a pull of what I imagined to be a huge perch.

To this day I remember the great thrill of feeling the rod top bow to the dash of what I felt sure was an enormous fish, and the thrill was intensified when something bright and silvery leapt from the water attached obviously to my tackle.

A call to my father for help brought hm quickly to my side, but in response to my appeal to him to take the rod, I was told : " No, you hooked the fish and you must kill it."

My knowledge of playing a fish was primitive, but the tackle held and the fish was brought eventually to the gangway side, where my father slipped the landing net under a trout, a bare two-pounder but well over the killable limit of those days—over sixty years ago—which was twelve inches in length or 1 lb. in weight.

Thus was my first trout caught, and a Thames trout angler born.

The passage of time has not lessened the thrill that comes when a trout well and truly grabs my spinning bait, and the killing of some hundreds of fish has brought as many hundreds of such joys to add spice to the beauties of scenery and climate which almost necessarily are associated with this fascinating branch of angling.

Being mainly a recitation of personal reminiscences these chapters will contain " I," " me " and " my " in profusion, for which I must ask my readers' to show forbearance and to exonerate me from a charge of boastfulness or of undue egotism.

"THAMES" TROUT.

This is a broad application in reference to the trout of the Thames.

That there were trout in the river hundreds of years ago is highly likely, and that they had distinctive features a possibility, but I have never seen, and know not, if such things exist as specimens mounted say, one hundred years ago.

In the days of my youth restocking the Thames was more or less in its infancy, but in the past sixty years, or even more, great numbers of trout in various stages of growth, from fry to four-pounders and upward, have been introduced from other waters to our beloved Thames.

It is quite likely that some of the fish I have mounted in cases and blatantly labelled "Thames" Trout, first saw the light in Scotland, or Norwich, or one of the rivers Exe, Kennet, Severn or Wick.

Apart from other associations which have put "foreign" trout in the Thames, the little Preservation and Restocking Association of Henley has been instrumental in introducing, since 1883, upwards of 12,000 trout, ranging in size from yearlings to good fish of four pounds and over in weight.

A fair proportion of these fish came from ova procured from one of the above-named sources, afterwards hatched at Colstrop near Hambleden, and kept penned in nursery until large enough to be put in the main river.

Unfortunately the hatchery had to be abandoned owing to (1) lack of funds, (2) the stream becoming intermittent and consequently unsuitable for reasonably safe work.

In addition to the above, 11,000 Loch Leven fry were bought and put down, and the ova dealt with, between and including the years 1883-8, numbered 172,000.

In the years 1905-6 250 trout up to 14½ inches in

length were marked with silver tags and put down in
the Henley Reach, The capture of a few of these fish
was reported, one as far downstream as Bell Weir, another
upstream at Tilehurst, and I caught one between Hambleden and Hurley, nearly opposite Medmenham Abbey ;
the first-mentioned was the largest and weighed about
$2\frac{1}{2}$ lb.

In 1906 one of the trout-breeding establishments made
a present to the Henley Association of twenty-five *Salmo
fontinalis*, a variety that has distinctive markings.

These were put in the tail-water of New Mills near
Henley, and in the following year I caught one when
barbel fishing. This fish weighed, on spring balance, just
under 2 lb., and was returned to the water. About eight
years later a local angler was spinning over the weeds for
pike at Medmenham and caught a trout of 7 lb. 2 oz.,
which had the fin markings peculiar to *fontinalis*, and I
feel confident that this fish was one of those turned down
at New Mills. It was mounted and the case was inscribed
" Thames Trout," but unfortunately the case became
somewhat dilapidated and the fish moth-eaten, and it
was eventually destroyed. These were the only two of
the twenty-five of which evidence as to their presence in
the river was forthcoming. From the foregoing it
becomes evident that not every trout caught in the
Thames is a Thames Trout proper, also that fish turned
down at Henley Bridge do not necessarily re-stock local
reaches, but may benefit reaches many miles away both
up and down river. I believe, however—and have
almost convincing proof—that the majority of large stock
fish of 2 lb. to 4 lb. and upwards, when turned down in
an extensive weir-pool, take up what may be termed
permanent quarters, there being in such places ample
food supply, deeps and shallows, fast and sluggish water.

It has often given me much amusement when I have

had retailed to me such remarks as : " Of course he catches a lot of trout, he knows where he puts them in " !

That there are very large trout in the river is indisputable, and the old story of the biggest fish getting away is often true.

On both points my own knowledge is positive. I happen to be a good judge of the weight of fish, and in the salmon season make a hobby of judging the weight of such fish when lying on the local fishmongers' slabs. The managers of these establishments would corroborate my statement that almost invariably my estimate of weight is not more than a few ounces out either way, and is frequently correct, so that I feel sure that my word will not be doubted when I state that I have seen at least six trout of the 15 lb. to 20 lb. class in the Upper Thames. Of these the highest up-stream was at Mapledurham, and this fish I judged would scale 16 lb. to 18 lb. It was once hooked and brought up to the weir apron, made a sudden rush and rounded a stanchion, breaking the gut instantly. Sheppard, the very trustworthy professional, now dead, told me of this incident and named the weight which I have already suggested. Some years later, when my friend, Patrick Chalmers, leased the pools, a huge trout was seen to rise and seize a small fish that was being brought to the net ; this monster was said to be a twenty-pounder, and most likely was the fish hooked and lost by Sheppard's client. Almost the last time I fished Mapledurham, eight or nine years ago, a trout which at some time in its life had been a very heavy specimen, came twice at my spinning bait, missing it each time. This fish had an enormous head, and was very long, thin and dark, and I believe must have been going blind, or possibly was blind in one eye. In the same year Patrick Chalmers saw what must have been the same fish, in the same spot, as his description not only of the fish but of the way it came at his bait, tallied exactly with my own experience.

Another very big fish lived in the reach between Caversham and Sonning, but I saw this fish only once. Two were in the deep quiet water between Henley Bridge and Hambleden Lock, the larger fish having a distinguished neighbour in the person of the late Lord Hambleden, opposite whose tennis courts " Jumbo " apparently lived. I saw this fish on two occasions, both times my tackle being at home, it being barred on picnic days with my family. Never when I went to try for him did I see a sign that a trout was in the river ! Another very large fish lived a little below Medmenham Abbey lower boundary, and the late Bob Young and I had an excellent view of him, or her, one day by way of an extraordinary happening. We were dropping quietly down-stream and I was putting up a rod, when this trout rose, chasing a large bleak, which went straight from the middle of the river in a series of " long hops " toward a cattle drinking place, shelving gradually from deep water to a sand-bank. The speed of the chase was so great that the huge trout ran himself into such shallow water that he lay for some seconds flopping partly in sand, partly in water, and we had a wonderful view of him. Bob said, " That's an eighteen-pounder, sir," and I agreed with him. Bob was a trustworthy judge. On subsequent outings we put in many hours trying to catch this beauty, but never saw him again until one sunny, warm day in early March, when roach fishing near his home, where he may be to-day for all I know to the contrary.

The biggest of all lived in very deep quiet water above Hurley and was hooked on a trailed spoon and brought to boat by one of the sons of the late Rev. F. T. Wethered, who was the Vicar of Hurley. In a *Fishing Gazette* of the period—I believe 1893—was published a short account of the hooking and losing of this fish. Unfortunately I have no copy, but I have distinct recollection that the two anglers involved in the incident agreed that the trout was at least a twenty-pounder.

In the following season an angler with Bob Young had a first-class chance of catching this fish, but unfortunately ignored Bob's advice and failed to stick in the hook, thus missing the trout of a lifetime.

This fish was again hooked some years later, in February by a pike angler ; it rushed across the river almost from bank to bank, but the angler's line, shorter than it should have been, was run entirely out, and the trout broke away.

For some years afterwards it was occasionally seen at dusk, and was heard after dark leaping and falling back to the river, " like a man falling in the water " was the description given by a workman who lived in a cottage near the haunt of the fish.

I feel quite confident that this trout was fully a twenty-pounder, as one summer day, when I was picnicking with my family on the bank opposite his home, he leapt clear of the water and gave me an excellent view of his magnificent proportions.

A few lines about some heavy trout of which I have more or less intimate knowledge may here be usefully introduced.

So many stories of huge fish have been circulated which bear no seal of authenticity that it is well to have records as nearly as possible correct.

The heaviest that I have known to survive the test of balance scales and weights weighed some hours after it was killed 17 lb. 3 oz., and I saw this fish in a fishmongers' shop at Maidenhead in the year 1898. It was a thousand to one chance by which I heard of this fish, and immediately after " getting the tip " I set out to see it, hoping that I would not arrive too late.

This trout was caught by a workman in the neighbourhood of Radcot, the tackle used being a night line baited with lob-worms, with the object of catching eels. Diligent enquiry failed to get me in touch with the poacher, who quite naturally took every precaution to cover his tracks. Although his one slip of the tongue to a pal, a river man I knew rather well and himself not too scrupulous in his ways of catching fish, gave me the clue to the approximate locality and method of capture, neither inducement nor threat enabled me to get a correct history of the tragedy. The trout was sold whole to a " London gentleman," and that was all the information I was vouchsafed, an air of mystery clouded the whole incident, and the old jibe about honour among thieves was well illustrated.

In the year 1897 a grand trout of 17 lb. was netted from the Thames tideway and was taken by the fisherman to Alderman Nuttall of Kingston, who weighed the fish and put it in the river at Kingston.

There are records supporting these details which were related to me by a Kingstonian, now dead.

The Reading trout of 16 lb. 15 oz. has often been referred to as a Thames fish, but it was caught in the Kennet near a big brewery, the successful bait being a Wagtail, and the successful angler a local professional.

Reading Museum has a fine cast made by the late Frank Buckland of this fish, and details existed in the minute book of the Reading Angling and Preservation Association, of which my old friend, the late Fred Brown, was Hon. Sec.

Some years ago I endeavoured to trace this minute book after the dissolution of the R.A. & P.A., but was unsuccessful.

The best two trout caught by fair angling, and about which no doubt exists are a fifteen-pounder by the late Mr. Bob Shaw at Marlow, and one of 14 lb. 9½ oz. by the late Mr. Forbes at Chertsey.

Many well authenticated fish of 13 lb. down to 10 lb. have been recorded, and I am entirely convinced in my view that many equally good fish are in the river, particularly in the quiet main streams.

WHERE TO SEEK A LARGE TROUT.

The neighbourhood of an extensive eddy is always a very favourable spot, and most of the biggest fish I have known lived in such a locality.

The trout is likely to be just outside the eddy in a gentle stream, and often behind some kind of shelter such as a bank of weed, submerged bough, large boulder, end of a rush bed, or hole in the river bed.

The quiet water of the eddy usually holds a plentiful supply of food in the form of small fish of various kinds, and foraging is made easy to a hungry trout.

Any eddy, however small, in which bleak may be seen rising is always worth fishing, and the trout is usually risen or hooked a few yards outside the eddy.

A good area of water above and below an island or rush bed should always be carefully fished, also the neighbourhood of an overhanging tree where bleak congregate.

When one has some knowledge of the bed of the river, or when a stranger notes a boily stream, the water below the boil should always be closely fished, there generally being a hole in which a trout may live.

Minnows and fry congregate behind the piles of camp-sheathing and it is fairly certain that trout patronize such larders.

The spot where one has caught a trout in the open water is always worth fishing again after an interval of a few days or weeks as another fish will probably take its place, particularly if there be a pronounced hold or shelter.

A ten-pound trout that I caught on the edge of a large eddy contained seventeen gudgeon ; apart from these the fish disgorged nine when being brought to landing-net.

About Some Trout I Have Caught.

From the time of catching my first trout I propose to make a jump of ten years to 1890, when I began to keep a record of my captures. With the exception of the usual vacations, school and subsequent studies much curtailed my angling excursions in those ten years, but being one of those fortunate people to whom long hours of sleep are not essential, I managed to get a great deal of early morning fishing, which otherwise I could not have enjoyed.

Many scores of times have I been on the river by the regulation hour before sunrise, and on one such memorable occasion caught four *killable* trout before returning to my home for breakfast. I had, and still have, the gift of being able to awake at any given hour, and on the only occasion I put my faith in an alarm clock it let me down, much to my chagrin, as I had an appointment with my old friend the late C. H. Cook (John Bickerdyke). However, my luck was in, for although I was half an hour behind the appointed time in reaching my punt, my friend did not put in an appearance until twenty minutes later, full of apologies. Having suitably pulled his leg I confessed to having been half an hour late myself, so all was well.

That morning I had the pleasure of taking him to, and landing for him, a 6 lb. trout, one of two which I had seen feeding on the edge of a deep hole, the other caught by me the following season being larger.

In fifty-five years, including 1945, it has been my

pleasure to catch 878 trout over 3 lb. each, and a large number over the 16-inch limit and up to 3 lb. Of these I have ten mounted whose average weight was 9¾ lb. In addition to these, 56 ranging between 6 lb. and 8 lb. 13 oz. came to my landing net. In 1941 my trouting days were seven, and the result four trout—7 lb. 10 oz., 6 lb. 14 oz., 2½ lb., and 2 lb., the two small ones being given " another chance."

In 1945 my bag was eleven, of which six were killed, the best brace being 8 lb. 13 oz. and 7 lb. 14 oz., and the smallest fish 2½ lb.

My rule to keep no trout under 3 lb. has rarely been broken, and then only when badly hooked—a very infrequent happening—or to keep a promise to a friend.

Many fish over 3 lb. and up to 5 lb. have been returned to the river, and this could be verified at the time of penning these lines by a number of people who have witnessed the operation. Unfortunately I am compelled to refer to many old friends and acquaintances as " the late."

The great majority of the large fish were caught in the open river, away from the weirs, which—generally speaking—are nowadays (prior to the war) over-fished by anglers using unsuitable gear.

My best year's fishing yielded thirty fish over 3 lb. ; this was forty-six years ago. Two other years each gave me twenty-nine fish.

Some Good Days.

Six between Whitchurch and Mapledurham, best 8½ lb., all caught on natural bait, chiefly bleak spun on Thames flight.

Five between Hambleden and Marlow, best 6 lb.

Five between Caversham and Shiplake, best 7 lb. 2 oz.

Eight on two occasions at Mapledurham, from 17 in. up to 5 lb. ; five only of the sixteen killed.

Three in one evening at Shiplake, best 6 lb. 5 oz.

Three or four in one day on several occasions.

CHAPTER II

1934—EXTRAORDINARY

THIS was an extraordinary year, in which I did a considerable amount of early morning and evening fishing, principally at weirs between and including Marlow and Mapledurham ; this was on account of a long spell of low water after April, making open river fishing almost useless from lack of stream and plentitude of weed. My total catch was forty-eight, of which only sixteen were 3 lb. or larger. Fifteen were caught in April, five killed ; eighteen in May, four killed ; in June and July I fished 15½ hours and caught four fish, 3¼ lb., 3 lb., 17 in. and 15 in. August 18 hours, eight trout, best 6¼ lb., spinning small gudgeon. September 13½ hours, three trout, best 4¼ lb. Of the forty-eight fish, fourteen were killed, thirty-nine were 16 in. or over, and nine under 16 in. Many were caught on a thinly-dressed fly which, when worked, looked like a "tiddler," on which the trout appeared to be feeding. On April 29th, I fished all day without seeing a rise or feeding fish. June 1st, in three hours out fishing two good trout in the 5 lb. or 6 lb. class came for my spinner, one plucked the gudgeon clean off my Thames flight, the other came short, was lightly hooked and leapt out of the water and off the hook in less time than I have been writing the last two lines. In this season a great many small trout were caught by other anglers, few being over 2½ lb.

About Some Trout I Did Not Catch.

The biggest trout it has been my lot to hook was undoubtedly well on in the 'teens, and this fish gave a good illustration of the fact that it is not always a big fish that makes a big splash, and vice versa.

The scene of the eventual tragedy was Marsh Weir, and the time about 8.15 in early May. My bait was becoming rather ragged with wear and I was winding it in on the edge of some quiet water. intending to renew it, when a fish rose very quietly to it, making a very small ring in the water, took hold and plunged powerfully down to the depths. I realised at once that I had hooked an outsize fish, and recalled that in the preceding year I had been told by an angler new to the Thames that he had seen a " huge trout " which came at his artificial spinner and broke away. Having known three or four pound trout termed " huge," " enormous," " monster," etc., by newcomers to the river, I did not follow up the angler's remark as to size, but merely advised him to avoid further use of a split ring as part of his fishing gear. The trout I had hooked kept well down, pulling hard and working in a large sweep, and the hardest strain I dared to use seemed to make no impression on the strength of the fish. This continued nearly a quarter-of-an-hour before I was able to bring him near the surface, and when this happened I saw about half his fan before he headed again for the 20 ft. depth, quite enough for me to see that I had hooked the trout of a lifetime. The fight went on stubbornly for several more minutes, the trout coming up once again, before being sufficiently under control to be brought toward the waiting landing net in the hands of the lock-keeper to whom I had given instructions : " Don't be in a hurry " and " Don't lift the net until I tell you." In spite of these words, and to my horror, when a little more than a foot of the head and shoulders of the trout came over the net, the netsman lifted, the fish slid back, a hook caught in a mesh, and the trout was free, the hook-hold had given way, no breakage. As the great fish flopped slowly away on its side down-stream, I could see every inch of his length and magnificent depth. Some seconds elapsed before the fish righted and sank quietly to deep water, whilst I stood too speechless even to curse the lock-keeper. When eventually I asked : " Why did you lift before I told you ? " the reply was : " I'm very sorry, Sir, I thought he was over the net." My vocabulary being unequal to the occasion, I merely said : " You have lost me the fish of a lifetime and yourself a sovereign."   It is true that the biggest fish does get away—often. It is also true that the incident upset me to the extent that I—one of the " keenest-ever " trout-fishers—felt no inclination for more than a week to take out a rod.

GUT SUBSTITUTE.

In 1914 I was persuaded by a friend to try a gut substitute, a material that appeared to be good, and on test in length gave all the answers satisfactorily. With this material I tied some spinning traces, four in all, and on one of them caught a brace of trout, approximately 9 lb. On the next occasion before using this trace I examined it carefully and found every knot and strand apparently perfect. I had seen a big trout which I estimated would go about 12 lb., in a weir stream not far from Reading, and set out to try to catch this fish. I nearly did. How nearly I will tell you, dear reader. I had fished for and rested this fish about 3½ hours, and pack-up time was fast approaching. For what was to be my last bait of the evening I mounted a dace on Thames flight and following my usual practice, spun fast six casts over and around what I judged to be his " lie." Nothing happened. Ten minutes rest and I made the first of my last six—and one for luck—casts, still spinning fast. The trout came for my bait with a very hard strike, hooking himself, as a trout frequently will, without the help of the angler's strike. Playing him, or he playing me, was all carried out true to specification, and I was standing on a convenient block with the landing net at the ready under my left arm to bring to instant action, whilst I was making the last few winch turns to draw the trout within reach. A yard from the rim of the extended net it happened ; something gave way and the trout lay motionless a moment, than swung round with a tail smack on the surface of the water and was gone. A knot had slipped at a swivel, although it had stood much more tension in the playing of the fish than was being applied when drawing him towards the net. The remainder of the trace and the three unused ones followed the trout into the depths of the pool, and I vowed never again to be seduced from good honest silkworm gut.

FOR TWENTY-FIVE YEARS.

That vow stood good, but in 1939, such is the power of pushful advertisement, I again fell for a substitute for silkworm gut, said to be marvellous. It was, to look at, and in tests gave no disappointments. It was the last day of August and nearly the end of the season, river very slack, clear and weedy, no use for open river fishing. It was a very warm day, one of those days on which trout will rise from the depths of a weir pool and lie a yard or so under the surface.

The substitute under notice needed no soaking, so said the books, but to tighten things up I put my cast in a damper-box before mounting it for use with a live-bait tackle. On this livebait tackle I put a medium-length bleak, and floated it down to the site of the greatest depth in the pool, where I allowed it to work quietly as it willed. To shorten my yarn I will say that eventually a large trout took the bait and going quietly away was " hit " sufficiently hard to stick in the hook, and I hold the opinion that a hook " struck " in puts more " near breaking " strain on tackle than that applied in killing a fish, if the killing be properly done. Anyway, I obeyed all the rules of playing a fish, learned from my A.B.C. days of trout fishing to the day under notice. The fish had made a number of strong runs, and at times was under quite considerable strain to keep it away from dangerous spots, and was well under control. In the middle of what apparently was going to be one of it last few runs, making steadily without any jigging for the middle of the pool and under quite moderate strain, suddenly the rod straightened and Fario departed almost unseen. I saw part of his back once, and the lock-keeper—handy with the net—saw his length in the sunlight, and making due allowance for enthusiasm he was a big fish. All the cast with the exception of the top loop went with the fish, and although on first inspection and test every knot seemed to be perfect, examination of the loop under a powerful glass revealed a nick caused by knife or scissors in the trimming. I have fished very little since August, 1939, but it has been always with silkworm gut, which is quite good enough for me.

JUST ONE MORE—AND THE SEQUEL.

On a Sunday morning in mid-May I reached Bob's (Young) punt at Medmenham after facing a stiff and cold North-Easter—a part of Buchan's cold spell—on my

HAMBLEDEN WEIR. WHERE THE $6\frac{1}{2}$LB. TROUT WAS CAUGHT,
AND A LOST SPINNING FLIGHT RECOVERED

PART OF THE OLD WEIR AT MARSH, WHERE MY FIRST
TROUT WAS CAUGHT

WHERE—IN EARLY JUNE—THE TEN POUNDER WAS CAUGHT

HENLEY BRIDGE. WHERE THE SEVEN POUNDER LEAPT INTO
A PUNT

6 mile cycle ride from Henley to find that usually genial soul looking rather glum and disgruntled. Finding that nothing worse than the weather was upsetting him, I gave him some consolation by reminding him that we had caught trout on worse days. He then told me that two days previously he had enjoyed a good view of a trout I had seen chasing a dace a fortnight earlier. As the fish had not shown himself I had no idea of his size, but the length of the dace he was bent upon eating indicated a " goodish " one.

Pulling Bob's leg, I said " Another of your ten-pounders, I suppose, Bob." " Yes, that he is, Sir," replied Bob, " he ran a roach half way across the river and caught him under the oak tree, then in turning jumped clear out of the water, he is nearer 12 lb. than 10 lb." " Right ho ! Bob, if you say so I am satisfied." With such a wind strongly blowing there was not much to choose from in the way of finding a sheltered spot, together with the chance of running a trout, so we decided to try the vicinity of the oak tree near which is a deep ballast hole between an up-stream and a down-stream hill.

The punt was moored by a single weight and kept steady by a rypeck about twenty yards above the up-stream drop into the hole, and following my usual practice in such circumstances, I began spinning the reachable area of water fan-wise, my first cast being to the right, and the bait a freshly killed dace mounted on Thames flight. Covering the whole area yard by yard and finishing with a cast to my right-angle left, I rested the water about half an hour, (meanwhile Young and myself), keeping as sharp lookout as could be in such rough conditions for a sign of a feeding fish. This procedure continued until about 1.30 when we began to feed on our favourite lunch of cold sausage, hard new crust and Cheddar accompanied by " good old beer " thoughtfully procured by Young

Saturday evening. The latter was most welcome as
the May North-Easter can be—and was—very keen.
Nearing the finishing point, Bob suddenly exclaimed
Look, Sir ! " I promptly looked, and saw a dace making
very quick time in the direction of the oak tree. The
dace was last seen in almost exactly the spot where Bob
had seen the big trout clear the water, and a big splash
indicated that the fugitive had found his last home.
Different spinning tactics were now essential, and my
first cast was as straight and as far down mid-stream
as the awkward wind would allow. This cast was followed
by alternate casts to right and to left and at the sixth
cast I experienced that thrilling moment which comes
when a big trout seizes a spinner. To shorten my story
I will say simply that the fish fought long, hard and deep,
never once showing until the last minute. The great
moment for using the landing net was imminent and
Bob was standing at the ready, the fish coming slowly
up to the surface and across the stream. A couple of
yards from the net the spent fish turned on his broad side
and at the same moment the rod suddenly straightened
and a game and magnificent trout was free. We were
flabbergasted as the strain on the tackle was much less
than it had been at times in course of the fight, but the
flight appeared when lifted from the water to be perfect.
Examination showed that the lip-hook which was of the
pattern in common use in those days had opened and the
turn-over of the trout must have given just that fraction
of variation of direction of pull sufficient to release the
hook, neither of the triples having been engaged. The
day ended blank, but my loss gave me food for thought,
and I evolved a new method of tying a Thames flight
which has never let me down.

CHAPTER III

THE SEQUEL:—"RUBBING IT IN"

SOME months later I was pike fishing with Bob and the water being somewhat discoloured was using a single hook paternoster baited with a large gudgeon. Fifty yards above and below the oak tree is good for pike in high water, and we had four nice fish in the punt when nearing lunch time. I was just lifting the paternoster preparatory to searching fresh water when my bait was seized with a violent pull and the fish went straight away out from the slack into the stream. I turned to Bob saying : "This is no pike, Bob," and it wasn't, for after a tough fight Bob slipped the landing net deftly under —presumably—our friend of May. He—or she—was hooked just in the edge of the upper jaw and was easily unhooked. As the fish lay on the floor with nose up to punt side Bob scratched a mark at the end of his tail and carefully put him back in the river unhurt and strong. His length was $28\frac{1}{2}$ inches, which in high season would mean for Thames trout a weight of at least $11\frac{1}{2}$ or 12 lb., so Bob's judgment was vindicated. He was a young, small-headed and thick fish, almost salmon silver with very few spots, but we never had another offer from him although we tried a number of times in the best part of the following season.

LUCK.

If there is one question more than any other that annoys me when I am fishing it is to be asked . "Have you had any luck ? " I am not asserting that there is *no* luck in fishing, having had spots of it myself, but there is one thing I positively assert and that without any hesitation or qualms. It is that luck does not make a successful angler, if only for the reason that luck is not consistent ; it will be found that the most successful anglers year in and year out are those who know their job thoroughly yet never are above learning, sometimes from unlikely and unpromising sources and subjects. There is the well-known hunter's instinct, and equally, although not often recognised, angler's or fisherman's instinct. A very great deal depends upon observation and study in this as in most other pursuits, and in fishing for trout on the Thames I owe to those qualities more than one brace of good fish. One small example will suffice to illustrate my point.

Not very far from my late home at Shiplake is a length of bank that is very low, and between that bank and the small footpath is a length of hollow. Walking this path one evening looking for a moving trout, I saw in the hollow a bleak not yet dead ; as a matter of fact it swam away when put in the river. My flight being already mounted I did not need another bait as dusk was almost due. I had never known of a trout at this particular spot, although after high water it was and is a likely lie, but knowing no other Thames fish that can chase and make a bleak leap nearly so fast and so far as can a trout, I judged that one had quite recently been working the vicinity. I spun out my first stand of six casts without result, but at the third cast of my second stand down stream was rewarded by a lovely strike which resulted in my landing a good trout of 7 lb. 12 oz. But I am digressing and must return to " luck." I am indebted to an unremembered author for the following quotation for which I give him my thanks without offering an apology for using it, as it is so much worth while.

"I don't say there's no such thing as luck—good and bad : but it ain't the explanation o'success an' failure—not by a long way. No, sirree, luck's just the thing any man'd like to believe is the reason for his failure and another feller's success. But it ain't so. When another man pulls off what you don't, the first thing you got ter believe is it's your own fault : the last, it's his luck. An' you jus' got ter wade in an' find out whar you went wrong, an' put it right, 'thout any excuses an' explanations."

SOMETHING ABOUT CATCHING THEM

SPINNING.

From *Angling* by ROBERT BLAKEY, 1884.

"Weybridge is about 20 miles from the Metropolis, and is an excellent locality for genuine fishing purposes. Trout are often pretty plentiful.

"At the time we are penning these lines we have seen a capture of this fish made on an angling excursion, by C. Alfred Junr. of 54, Moorgate Street, City, which is a splendid specimen of Thames trout-fishing.

"His creel contained thirteen fish in all ; one was *twelve and a half pounds*, one *seven*, and one *five* pounds ; and the remainder were of more than average size. (No trout to be killed of less weight than one pound was then the law, A.E.H.)

"These were caught by an artificial bait (an imitation of a small gudgeon manufactured by himself), by trolling.

"Two of these fine fish are now preserved, and may be seen at the above fishing-tackle establishment.

"Such an exploit as this shows that the trout must have now become pretty numerous in the river."

C

The above cutting is quoted mainly to indicate that
in all probability the trout were caught in the open
reaches of the river, where alone trailing or trolling could
be effectively performed, weir-pools and runs being unsuitable for the navigation of a craft for this method of
catching trout—I will not term it angling or fishing—in
fact great danger of shipwreck would be courted by
attempting to navigate the most likely trout holds of
such water.

Trolling, trailing or harling—it was often called spinning—was largely indulged in prior to 1894 when it was
made illegal by a Bye-law in the Thames Conservancy
Act, which (No. 5) reads :—" No person or any vessel
under way upon the Thames shall draw or cause or
suffer to be drawn in the direction in which such
vessel is proceeding any line with hook or bait attached
thereto, whether such line be attached to a rod or
otherwise."

I have somewhat laboured the foregoing quotation
and comment for two reasons. The first to show that
60 years ago the open streams yielded a considerable
number of trout, as they would to-day if more consistently
fished ; and the second to emphasize that trailing or
trolling is not spinning, the latter being an artistic
and skilful method of angling, whilst trailing or trolling can be carried out on waters, where it is not
barred, by the merest novice, the real art in each case
being the manipulation of the craft by the waterman
or gillie."

There are several good books obtainable which deal
exhaustively with this fine art, and the following lines do
not pretend to give more than brief outlines and hints
pertaining to the particular river and fish under notice.
For example, I have nothing to say about thread line
spinning other than the fact that I have never used this

method on Thames. It may be quite good, probably is in the hand of an expert, but my preference is fixed in another direction which has yielded a large number of fish, and sustained an amazingly small proportion of breakages. I have recollection of an angler using thread line who told me—not without some pride—that he had run five trout, but " they all broke me up." As a scientific style of angling the art of spinning when thoroughly understood is unbeaten by any other form of fishing, dry-fly—about which I am not entirely ignorant—not excepted.

There is much that can be learned only by experience, observation and judgment, and by profiting by one's mistakes. In the early part of the season when as a rule the weather is not too warm, a day's spinning from the bank is a real joy to me, this is not only due to the fact that I am trying to catch one of the most beautiful of fishes, but to the added delight of seeing Nature unfolding herself in many wonderful ways. The gentle exercise of traversing perhaps three or four miles of riverside, noting the particular stage of growth of foliage and vegetation as compared with other years, and observing the ways of bird and animal life all go to convince one that there is much more in fishing than catching fish. In regard to bank spinning I am convinced that far too little of this is done by the average trout-fisher. There is a much bigger head of trout in the open river than in the weir-pools, and an infinitely larger number of these fish have escaped being hooked and lost than in the weirs, where the majority of anglers fish, consequently the trout are less shy. Given the ability to mount and spin a bait properly, the bank spinner has a greater chance of sport than the puntsman or weir fisher. On a number of occasions when the bleak were up I have seen four or five trout feeding at the same time, and the late Bob

Young and George Lumsden both told me they had seen in their repective reaches as many as six moving at the same time, a statement that I had no hesitation in believing. The average weight of fish caught in the open water is much higher than that of weir-caught trout. Most of the open water fish live in the same spot or quite near it—depending upon the height of the water—practically all the year round, only a small proportion of them working up to the weirs in very low water, and using generally the nearest to home gravel shallow at spawning time. I have often been asked which is the best part of the Thames on which to spin for trout, but have always expressed the opinion that there is no best part. Every reach holds its share of good fish, and in the days of my youth when a great deal of open river fishing was done, one heard of large trout being caught at Hampton Court Shepperton, Maidenhead, Marlow, Medmenham, Henley, Sonning, Tilehurst, Wallingford, Sandford and Oxford ; it would be the same these days if more people fished the same reaches—not the weirs. I remember some three years ago a correspondent to *The Fishing Gazette* expressing some surprise that he had caught a trout by spinning in the open river—I believe near Windsor—and had run one or two more on spinning bait. My surprise is that so many men crowd to the weirs. I have known nineteen attempting to fish at one time from one weir on the Upper Thames, a state of affairs which made it impossible for any part of the water to be effectively fished. May I be forgiven for quoting the following lines from an article written by me some years ago, and published in one of the sporting journals, which I cannot remember.

" Where to spin on any particular reach can be determined by knowledge—local and general—observation and ' fisherman's instinct.' Local knowledge is very useful but not necessary, but general knowledge is indispensable ; observation is a strong hand that leads to success, but that indescribable faculty which for want of a better term I call fisherman's instinct is the master card." Most of the foregoing is not " spinning " but it convincingly brings me to the principal point of spinning, namely, that an angler able to cast a clean 35 or 40 yards, which is a moderate length of line, and on occasion, can make 50 or 60 yards is well on the way to success on open water. Accuracy in judging distance and in reaching a certain spot are adjuncts to running a fish, and can be acquired by practice. Generally it is good to spin fast, a feeding trout is a very fast mover. Spin very fast for fifteen to twenty turns of the winch, slow down for ten or twelve turns, then revert to fast and so on until the bait is near the bank, a following trout will often take a few yards from the rod point. On occasions the bait will be seized within the first few yards of its fall. Usually the pull is very strong and no strike is needed, and if given will result in a smash unless the tackle be very heavy. As to bait, my preference is a freshly killed bleak, gudgeon, or dace mounted on the Thames pattern flight, it should spin straight and true, without the wobble that is so attractive to pike. Preserved sprat, roach, bleak, dace, gudgeon and small eel tail are good, but cannot be mounted satisfactorily on a Thames flight, and one of the many patterns of fanned mounts should be used. The fault of a bait so mounted is its stiffness, which is absent from the all gut Thames flight and newly killed bait. Although the latter consists of three triples and a lip hook it is rare for more than one or two of the hooks to take hold, and since using my improved lip-hook I have caught many trout on this only. Even with the three triples and lip-hook it is not uncommon for a big trout to strip the bait from the flight without getting hooked ; how this is done I do not attempt to say but it has happened to me and to other persistent spinners a good many times in both slow and fast water.

Once in a weir-pool at Goring, and once in the open river near Medmenham I have had a gudgeon stripped clean off the flight by large trout of the ten-pound class.

In the weir pool my spinner was nearing the end of recovery from a long cast when I and the late Harry Young (Bob's brother), who was standing beside me, saw the great trout dash out from under the apron after my gudgeon, which he appeared to seize with the end of his jaws across the body, in a second the bait was off, and only a very slight pull felt ; had only one hook of one triple been in contact with the trout's flesh no strike would have been needed to fix the hook over its barb.

The second occasion was perhaps more interesting.

I was spinning from a high bank, using a gudgeon on my favourite Thames flight. Well out in the stream I felt a slight pluck, and immediately a large trout leapt clear of the water. The flight came to hand minus gudgeon, but otherwise intact.

Bob's remark was :—" It's a long dash mystery to me how they manage to do that ; I've seen it done before."

It is still a mystery to me.

This trout, a nine pounder, fell victim to a spun bleak about a fortnight later.

These two instances—I have experienced others—are mentioned just to show that it is not a question of a small fish merely fringing the bait, or of having a mouth with inadequate gape to engulf the gudgeon, for even a small trout can and will swallow a large gudgeon, bleak or small dace !

In April, 1896, spinning a gudgeon from the high bank near Magpie Island a mile or so below Hambleden Lock

I rose, and Young eventually netted, a trout of 5 lb. that was hooked just at the butt of his fan.

Although not large this fish was very old, with a big head like that of a cock salmon kelt, his lower jaw protruding much above the upper jaw, and curved like the prow of a canoe.

This happening set us—Young and me—theorizing, and we arrived at the conclusion, supported by a previous similar incident that had happened to an old client of Young, that on account of its deformity this fish could not approach and catch its bait in a normal way, and adopted means to disable its prey before grabbing it, this being effected by lashing at the fast swimming bait with its—the trout's—tail.

In attempting this manœuvre with my spinning bait foul-hooking resulted, also a fight out of all proportion to the weight of the fish.

Some years later our theory was visibly confirmed at Marlow Weir when both of us saw a 7¾ lb. trout knock my bleak a foot out of water then quickly turn and grab it ; this fish was as ugly as the one previously mentioned.

To my great regret Young is not alive to be able to confirm these stories.

On two occasions when spinning above a weir, once at Mapledurham, and once at Hurley I have had large trout rush like a flash down through the open sluice to the pool below, where each was netted ; the larger of the two weighed 9 lb. 5 oz., and how the kill was accomplished is related in the final chapter of this book.

Young experienced a similar incident when attending the late Col. Shipway of Henley ; the trout in this instance scaled 8 lb., and was landed at Hambleden Weir.

Artificial baits are legion, but of them all two are outstanding, Phantom and Wagtail. A blue Phantom in water that is slightly coloured is very killing and Wagtail runs this excellent bait very close ; it will be noted that both are soft.

In normal times there are spinning rods in plenty, and mainly it is a matter of personal choice, and the amount of money one is prepared to spend. A liberal allowance of the latter plus pride of possession may indicate a built cane at £10 that will give no better fishing results than a good " cleft " greenheart at less than half the cost. I have one of the latter that was built for me by the late David Slater, of Newark, close on fifty years ago, and it looks good for another half century, although it has killed a very large number of fish, but it has been used and tended carefully.

Ten or eleven feet is a good length, longer if you are a long man and like a long rod. It must not be stiff and it must not be whippy, the former will help to smash fine tackle, and the latter will not give good clean casting. Some anglers prefer a much shorter rod, but so many times have I found a 10 ft. or 10 ft. 6 in. rod useful in weir-fishing that I rarely use my nine-footer for other than open water spinning.

In weir-fishing an extra foot or eighteen inches means that one is able to hold a fish away from blocks or obstructions in places where a shorter rod would involve having the gut cut on a concrete edge, or broken round a pile or stanchion.

Rod building has in recent years been so carefully studied by good makers that such details as rings and winch fittings, etc., need not be discussed. As to the reel, I have seen none of the multitude of patterns of recent introduction better than a 3½ in. or 4 in. Aerial ; I own one of the earliest made, it is still very useful, but looks a very poor relation to the up-to-date pattern. A great charm of the Aerial is that it is not fool proof, thus in use calling for skill and concentration to avoid over-run with its consequent marvellous bird's nest of line ! As with the rod, careful attention is necessary to keep it in such condition as to give best results, cleaning and oiling should be regularly done.

The line I prefer is an eight or ten pounds breaking strain, very best quality silk, dressed, not because such a size is necessary to kill a big trout but on account of the frictional wear resulting from spinning. Nowadays the friction is reduced to minimum by the excellent types of rings available, but all the same a line of such type will outwear two or three of finer gauge ; also it will cast longer and cleaner than an undressed line, moreover, it can be used for casting from the reel, from a coil on the bank or punt floor, from loops depending from the left hand, and from figure of eight coiling in the hand when spinning fast water.

It should be not less than one hundred yards long and should be carefully dried after use if only half a dozen casts have been made. Naturally, it will wear and shorten by use, but I provide for this by having plenty of undressed back-line. A strong, heavy trout will make a very long run on occasions, and if weir fishing it may be impossible for the angler to follow and " cut off " his fish.

How to use the outfit ? After studying one of the aforementioned books, practise persistently either on the river or on a meadow oi your lawn. One of the commonest faults I see is forcing, or jerking the cast ; swing and correct timing will add yards to the cast, and these two essentials apply in spinning as much as in golf, rowing, fly-fishing and other exercises and pastimes.

CHAPTER IV

"LIVEBAITING"

USING a livebait and fishing with a livebait are
entirely different propositions. " Purists," who
affect to despise fishing with livebait, possibly have
never done it and therefore are unqualified to be dog-
matic. To fish a weir properly with livebait is a *whole
time job*, calling for considerable skill and complete concentration. To run a baited tackle down a weir stream,
put down the rod and leave the bait to do its own
searching is mostly futile, and calls for no skill. True,
it may find a trout or a trout may find it, but the odds
against such happening are very long. Further, there
are times and places when and where the use of spinning
tackle make for entire waste of time and energy if one
be out to catch a trout, and it is reasonable to infer that
to be the primary object in fishing. Moreover, the cream
of the season is of such short duration that it behoves
the angler to use the means of fishing best suited to the
hour and the place. Clear and calm water, with a bright
sun, rule out spinning the open river, no matter how
good the angler and how perfect his tackle ; in weir
fishing clear water usually means low water and these
in bright sunny weather are conditions greatly against
success. If one does move a fish, he is almost certain to
come short even if he will go to the extent of touching
after following a bait. Even with very fine livebait gear,
the same happening is likely, but in much lesser ratio, if
the bait be properly worked.

If correctly chosen, the rod used for spinning will suit
admirably for livebaiting, if any difference it should be

six inches to a foot longer. The same kind of reel should be used, and should hold at least one hundred yards of undressed silk line of 8 lb. breaking strain, on which it is better at all times to whip a loop to connect to the trace, a knot of any description tending to weakness. It is elementary to suggest that great care should be taken to keep all running gear in sound and unfrayed condition. The trace should be two or three yards of gut, or, if you will, gut substitute, fine and of best quality. Hooks, single for small bait, a lip hook and one triple for medium, and lip hook and two triples for *large* bait, and do not jib at using a dace or roach six or eight inches in length. I have often seen trout chasing dace and roach of six or eight *ounces*, even larger. Weight will sometimes be needed on the trace and should be of saddle pattern, easily changed when necessary ; its size will depend on the water fished, and none is required in the open river or slow runs. A yard or so away from the bait will be found the most useful position, but on occasion two or three yards will be better, and on a gut trace should be folded over a knot. The cork that is used on live-baiting tackle is not a " float " as usually understood, but is an indicator to aid in working the bait to any required spot, and to show at all times exactly where one is fishing. It should be as small as possible, consistent with the eyesight of the user, and be shaped to offer as little resistance as may be to fast running water. In fishing some weirs it is not uncommon to hook a trout fifty or sixty yards from the rod point. My preference is for a piece of or a whole medicine bottle cork suitably trimmed and cut with a sharp pen-knife down its length to half its diameter, the advantage of this being if it becomes lodged in an obstruction it will frequently pull off without damage to the fine gut. As no two weirs run or can be fished alike, it would be futile to set out a definite way to work the tackle, but always it is essential to concentrate on judgment. At the same time there are points which should always be observed, and here are a few set out briefly : Cover every yard of water carefully, the piece you miss may be the very spot to hold a fish. Always keep the rod in hand ; if you want a rest wind up the tackle and keep the bait alive in a " safe " place. Keep the first thirty or forty yards of line greased, and on the surface so that it will lift quickly. Be constantly on the alert for a feeding fish, and get your bait in the vicinity of the rise as quickly as possible, a feeding trout is a very fast mover, but often moves methodically, starting from and catching his bait in or near the same spot several times in succession.

Take great care in striking to a run ; it often happens that a trout takes the bait with a tremendous pull, in which case he hooks himself, and to strike would be fatal to the tackle, if not to the fish. In the event of a fish taking in slack water or by crossing the stream, which often can be seen but scarcely felt, wind the line taut before firmly and without snatch sticking the hook in ; the mouth of a trout is very different from that of a pike. Make yourself as small and inconspicuous as possible, move quietly and without haste when going on, working, or leaving a weir platform. Before beginning to fish, make up your mind where you will land your fish if you hook one, and have an adequate landing net conveniently placed. Do not be discouraged by rough or cold weather if the water is right. I have caught trout in a bitter wind, in a snow-storm, and when hoar frost has whitened the grass. Do not become slack when such weather persists ; you may run a fish in the last half-hour of your day.

CHAPTER V

LOST AND FOUND

O N three occasions I have caught trout with tackle in their mouth that had been broken when the fish was previously hooked.

I will treat first with my own breakage and recovery.

Along the tumbling bays at Hambleden Weir some of the piles stand well above the surface of the water, and it is always good policy to try carefully behind each pile, as such a spot is always a likely lie for a feeding fish.

Early one morning a 6½-lb. trout rose at and seized my spinning bait and, instead of running down one of the side runs, which according to the rules he should have done, he deliberately dived almost vertically towards the depths of the pool.

This mean trick resulted in my spinning lead becoming caught in a crack in the top of the pile, and the gut snapped like cotton at the loop of the flight : my morning's fishing ended in my going home fishless to breakfast.

About 6.30 in the evening of the same day I began my fishing along the same tumbling bay, but knowing something of the strange ways of trout I avoided the spot where the fish was hooked in the morning, and began my spinning at the down-stream corner of the bay, where there was a very enticing run of water.

Details of my casting can be omitted, but in one of my periods of resting the run I saw a bleak leap twice before a splash indicated that either the bleak had escaped or was on its way down to the belly of the trout.

Soon after resuming spinning I hooked the fish, and

after a good fight—a five or six-pound fish often gives one a much livelier time than a bigger one—it was neatly landed by my old friend, the late Steve Bourner, the lock-keeper, who had been watching me from the lock.

One hook of the flight that I had lost in the morning was in the edge of the trout's jaw, and another in its gill-cover.

At Temple I caught a 5-lb. trout whose face was decorated with a 3-inch Wagtail, and at Mapledurham I landed on a Wednesday a good trout that had been lost on the previous Saturday by my friend the late Patrick Chalmers.

This fish fouled a pile in the lower—or mill—pool and was caught by me in the right-hand—or lock—pool.

As my friend had been compelled at a late moment to go to Town instead of joining me it gave me much pleasure to be able to return to him his tackle plus trout.

Unfortunately, it frequently happens that fish broken away with either spinning or live-bait tackle are so awkwardly hooked that they cannot feed, and if unsuccessful in rubbing out the hooks die of starvation.

SPEED AND AGILITY OF FEEDING TROUT.

The speed that a well-conditioned trout can work up when chasing a bleak or a dace is amazing, as also is the celerity with which he can change direction, or put on the brake.

This latter trait has cheated the landing-net of at least one outstanding fish. It happened at Hurley Weir pool. We knew that a big trout had his home in a very deep spot of the pool, and we had seen him a few times when he was after a large dace or a roach, but had never an opportunity to get in touch with him.

One very warm, bright and calm Saturday in early June, Young and I elected to sit on the weir platform, under the shade of the elder-tree, to eat our sandwiches, and I drifted a large live bleak over the area where most often we had seen the trout move. We were perfectly still and could see the bleak distinctly, and it had been in the same water within a few feet for over half an hour.

Bob suddenly exclaimed, " Look out, sir ! " I looked out without an instant's loss of time, and we saw a wave moving rapidly up-stream, also could plainly see the form of the big trout dashing for the bleak. We thought it a certainty that the bait would be seized and engulfed —a very thrilling moment for me—but when only inches from it the trout suddenly put on the brake and swerved to miss it, also by inches.

Examination of the bait and tackle disclosed nothing wrong other than a small piece of flannel-weed attached to the hook, and indiscernible from the weir ; the keen sight of a trout is wonderful.

There was no question of sun-glint from a polished gut trace, as in bright weather I invariably use some means of dulling the gut.

We waited two hours, and saw nothing more of that trout, but caught a small one, which was returned to the pool.

In the subsequent spawning season this fine trout was shot when on a redd in the spring that flows into the weir-pool, but unfortunately the fact did not come to light until long after it was too late to take action.

The slaughterer " mistook it for a jack," and " it pulled between 14½ and 15 lbs. on my steelyard," also " it kept us all in fish for nearly a week " : so said the miscreant, who was given a precise description of his character by both myself and Young.

A " Clappers " Trout.

On a Saturday afternoon in early May, when on my
way to try the " Clappers " or, properly, Caversham
Weir-pool, I called at a tackle shop in Market-place,
Reading, to buy certain leads.

Noticing my equipment, the shop assistant asked,
" Was I going trout fishing ? " On my reply that I was
just going, I was informed that I was just a week too
late if I was going to try to catch the big trout in the
Clappers."

Pursuing the interesting subject, I was told that for
two or three weeks a big trout pretty handy 10 lbs., had
been seen feeding at times in the pool, and old Bill ——,
Harry ——, and Mr. C—— and Mr. H—— had been
trying ever so many times to catch him, then last Saturday afternoon a gentleman from Henley, I think his
name is Mr. Hobbs, brought up his dinghy from Sonning
and saw the big trout feeding, and caught it only about
an hour after he got to the pool. " They " weren't half
grousing about it, too—" foreigners " coming to catch
their trout !

I asked the shopman if he had seen the fish after it
was caught, and was his story really true ? I was
assured that it was a fact, on which I commented, " You
have only one detail wrong, the trout was $8\frac{3}{4}$ lbs., not
10 lbs., but it was a lovely fish, one of the most beautiful
I have ever caught : here—producing a photograph—is
its picture."

" Are you Mr. Hobbs then, sir ? I do hope I haven't
said anything amiss," upon which I assured him that all
was well, and bade him good day.

One winter's day, when paternoster fishing for pike
in this pool (Clappers), I landed part of the steel frame

and rotten fabric of a carpet bag, probably a relic of one of the notorious late Mrs. Dyer's diabolical baby disposal orgies.

FLY-FISHING.

This mode of fishing—as usually understood—for trout in the Thames is not recommended, but there are circumstances and conditions in which it may be very successful with the smaller specimens. Exception may be made in the case of known fish which occupy the same beat constantly. On five occasions I have caught such fish, the best a 6½-pounder ; and an old friend, the late Dr. Shone, of Marlow, killed a fine fish of 8 lb. on a fly of his own invention, which is known as Shone's Fancy. It is mainly duck wing, with moderately full body and " gold " twist wrapping, and when worked probably has a family resemblance to a minnow. Best results from fly-fishing are to be obtained in weir pools and mill-tails when the river is low and clear, mostly late in May and throughout June. Curiously, even when the rise of fly is good in May, very few trout appear to become interested about it, but occasionally a fish may be found in one spot taking freely, and it has been my fortune to catch several such fish. In low, clear water, when the new season's fry are plentiful, a fly worked in the rippling light runs from lashers will prove successful.

Practically any thinly dressed pattern will do, the main object being to imitate as nearly as possible the small fry of which the smaller trout take big toll. As previously written, 1934 was an exceptionally good year for this type of fishing and I enjoyed excellent sport with smallish to medium weight fish, most of which were returned uninjured. As is well known, a 2 or 3-lb. fish will put up a great fight on fine tackle and a light fly-rod.

D

Usually my best results have been obtained in the evening of a very warm day, when the fry are well up in the water. A number of my friends who will do nothing but fly-fishing have been pleased with their experience on the foregoing lines.

CHAPTER VI

A TYPICAL—MORE OR LESS—DAY AFTER TROUT

AT breakfast on a Friday morning in an Easter vacation many years ago, a nephew suddenly fired this question at me : " When are you going out again, Uncle, to catch another trout ? "

My answer was, " I do not know ; I'll give up that one," but I added, " I intend taking the day off to-morrow to try to catch one."

Immediately my nephew asked, " May I go with you ? "

Noting my hesitation—for I knew that he was about as handy with a fishing-rod as I would be with a Spitfire —he exclaimed, " I don't want to fish ; I want to see you catch one."

That altered the matter, for I had taught the boy to become very useful with a pair of sculls, and his temperament was buoyant, almost incapable of boredom, particularly on the river.

I replied, " Very well, that will suit me ; you shall come."

" Where shall we go, Uncle ? " Knowing very well what the response would be, I told him that the skiff-punt was at Shiplake Lock, and the fishing punt at

Hambleden Lock, and he could choose for himself ; either way would suit my fishing. As I anticipated, he plumped for the Shiplake Reach, and incidentally the lighter craft ! I impressed upon him that he must be up for an early breakfast so that we could catch the 7.55 train to Shiplake, This concluded the arrangement for the time being.

In those days Easter weather was often very good, and the prevailing season was particularly fine and balmy, a dry spell had persisted for over a week, causing the river to run down to a lovely colour and favourable stream after a period of high water. All-round conditions appeared to be settled for the moment and I looked forward with some confidence—although wisely I did not say so to the boy—to catching one of a number of trout which I knew were in residence between Sonning and Shiplake.

The early morning of Saturday presaged another fine day ; we were up " bright and shiny " in time for a 7.15 breakfast, which " Auntie " had been enjoined to have ready punctually.

We caught the 7.55 with a few minutes to spare and reached Shiplake at 8 o'clock, following which we had a glorious spring morning ten minutes' walk to the Lock.

In passing, I would say that everybody pining for an extra hour of " summer-time " should get up an hour earlier in the morning, and abstain from tinkering with the clock.

The ever-reliable lock-keeper had mopped out the boat and shipped the gear, so no time was lost in pushing off.

The boy's mission was to scull gently up to Sonning Bridge ; mine was to rig up the rods and reels and put in soak the gut lines and traces likely to be needed in the day's outing ; further, and of more importance, to keep a sharp look-out for a feeding trout.

We proceeded placidly and without any trace of

excitement, there being scarcely a sign of fish life on the surface of the river until we were about a hundred yards from the head of the St. Patrick's Stream, when I saw a splash and big swirl in mid-stream. I immediately gave the agreed signal to the boy to hug the towpath bank until we were about sixty yards above where I had seen the swirl.

Here in mid-river I ordered the lowering of a seven-pound weight, just sufficient to hold the boat-head on in the absence of a strong breeze or stream, taking care to have at least three or four feet of slack line. To my boat I had made and fitted in the bow a cross-bar and short bowsprit of ash, detachable, and, when not rigged, occupying negligible space. To the end of the sprit was fixed a pulley which carried a light but strong sash-line, to which, when reeved over the pulley sheave, was attached the weight by means of a spring hook. To the starboard gunwale was fixed a cleat opposite the well thwart, so that when fishing alone I could manipulate the weight without walking the boat and causing a lot of disturbance.

The boat being steadied and all quiet, I proceeded to mount a small dace on a spinning flight, the boy watching the operation with much interest. Always in calm or very slightly ruffled conditions I prefer to cast from either a sitting or kneeling position ; it is easy when one has discovered how and has had plenty of practice.

Spun here, spun there—right, left and centre, my brilliant little bait attracted nothing, so after thoroughly covering the area I put aside the spinning gear and ran a live bleak downstream, moving the rod from side to side to cover as much water as possible.

Fishing all reachable water for a distance of about fifty yards downstream brought no rise after about half an hour's working, so *winding up slowly* I brought the bleak aboard, detached him and gave him his liberty.

I emphasize winding up slowly for a very good reason—often a trout will come at a thus moving bait, and I have caught more than one almost at the moment of lifting the bait from the water.

" We were too late for that one, old man. Up anchor and carry on. We will pay him another call on our way down. Often a trout that feeds at this time will feed again about six hours later. Scull up steadily ; there is no need to hurry."

A leisured and very pleasant journey brought us eventually to The White Hart landing stage, and not without ulterior motive I suggested to my young friend that a ginger beer might be acceptable after his labour ; from " labour to refreshment " is quite a good idea, and the man that invented it has a soft place in my heart.

Two ginger beers and two glasses of beer (that in those days was beer), minus the ginger, having made us feel much better, I explained to the boy that my programme was to spin from the bank—towpath—from the wooden bridge to a point about 150 yards downstream, then in the boat drop a little lower, moor above the barbel swim, and have lunch, meanwhile fishing a live bait, and keeping ready a spinning outfit. " Where there are barbel there is always a trout—sometimes two or three—this being because of the presence of a deep stretch, perhaps only a somewhat extensive hole below a shallow, or—Thames term—" hill."

" Would you like to prowl round the village and Lock for an hour or so or shadow me ? " Somewhat to my surprise, Jack chose the shadowing rôle, but I made no comment, although inwardly pleased.

Spinning down the bank produced no run other than from a pike of about 4 lb., which fortunately kicked free without damaging the flight when given slack line ; but

—again fortunately—a small trout between $2\frac{1}{2}$ lb. and 3 followed the spinning bleak to within three yards of the bank, when he saw danger and gave a very quick about turn. This little incident amused the boy and helped to keep his enthusiasm warm.

Arrived at the barbel swim, and having disposed the tackle and baits conveniently, the live bait working just over the point where the hill dropped to the hole, we settled down to dispose of a lunch for which I would not exchange one at a " posh " London restaurant, viz. : cold pork sausages, mustard, bread and butter, Cheddar cheese and crisp crust, banana and coffee ! It was a joy to see the boy do his piece !

The absence of tobacco may be noted, and in this connection some of my readers will be amused by the reason why. Some years before, when pike-fishing in the Henley Reach, I had finished my sandwiches and proceeded to light my pipe, my line meanwhile lying on the floor of the punt in two or three coils, lightly held from running with the stream by a small flat lead, easily moved without check if a pike ran with my pater-noster bait.

In striking a match off flew the head, alight, of course, and settled on the line, which I could not prevent from being burnt through. Although reasonably fluent, I was disgusted beyond words, and immediately threw the pipe overboard—it was a " bull-dog " clay—and vowed never to have another ! I haven't ! Neither do I smoke a whiff or a cigar when fishing from a craft.

Back to the barbel swim after that digression. Lunch finished, I devoted half an hour to working the live bleak in order to cover as much water as possible, then wound up and released the bait, still very lively and scarcely marked, as it should be if properly attached and carefully handled. My companion noticed that I dipped

my hand in the well of the boat before taking off the
bleak, and asked why I did so ; he was much interested
in my explanation that to handle with a dry, warm hand
a delicate fish such as a bleak or small dace would
probably strip it of a large number of its scales, and most
likely cause its death by setting up fungoid growth,
Mounting a gudgeon on the flight that had been hanging
over the boat-stern to keep trace and flight soaked ready
for instant use, I spun carefully over every yard of
reachable water without attracting a run, then decided
that on this particular day the barbel swim was not
going to provide my family with a trout dinner, nor my
collection of specimens with a " stuffer."

" Now, laddie, you may up anchor and drop quietly
down river, keeping about ten yards from the boughs ;
I want to spin all the water fairly close in, and all the
way down to where we first anchored this morning.
There we will put in an hour, and see if our friend is in
feeding humour."

Although admirable fishing conditions prevailed there
was no sign of a feeding fish, and the drop down to the
St. Patrick's Stream produced no run, not even from a
pikelet or perch.

Arrived at our mooring point, the weight was quietly
lowered, and I mounted a new spinning bait, I believe it was a gudgeon, intending to spin fanwise over
the whole reachable water, and repeat the operation,
perhaps twice.

My programme was cut short, for at the very first
cast there came that unmistakable pull that only a
good trout could give, but alas ! there was no resistance,
and I wound in the tackle to find the bait nearly stripped
from the flight, and hanging on only one hook near its
tail. Turning to the boy, I remarked : " That has put
paid to any further spinning here to-day."   Quite

properly I was asked, " How's that, Uncle ? "   My reply
that the trout had " seen enough of a spinning bait
to make him very careful " was perhaps understating the
matter, but having in the past persevered in spinning
after having had a similar snatch, and having never
caught a killable fish in such circumstances, I had a
fixed prejudice against persisting in spinning, so changed
the procedure and sent down a live dace.

Nearly an hour of searching the water, in the course
of which two alterations in the position of the boat
were made, brought no sign of a feeding fish, and as the
afternoon was slipping along apace, and there were two
more special places to which I wished to give a trial,
a move was made down to " Bromley's Bucks," always a
very likely trout-hold.   Incidentally, although called
" Bromley's Bucks," there are no bucks ;   they disappeared many years ago after eel-fishing by bucks
became unprofitable.

All the best of the water was spun over, the only fish
touched being a large chub, which almost engulfed the
bait, but was unhooked successfully and returned strong
and lively to the water.

" Now, my lad, we will drop to the head of that island
(" that island " being the second above Shiplake Lock).
Keep to port and lower the anchor in midstream about
fifty yards above that gate."   After carrying out my
instructions faithfully and well, and having had a few
minutes to take his bearings, my companion broke silence
by asking, " Why have you chosen this side of the island
when there is much more stream the other side ? "

" I have in mind four reasons, two of which are important ; the wind has almost died away, and, as you see,
the water over there is a flat calm on account of the
shelter of the island, and the sun is still bright, making
fishing conditions so much poorer now the river is clear.

A LARGE TROUT—8½LB.—PAST ITS PRIME
Note the Upturned Elongated Jaw

THE 1945 SEASON'S HEAVIEST RECORDED TROUT,
8LB. 13OZS. CAUGHT BY THE AUTHOR.

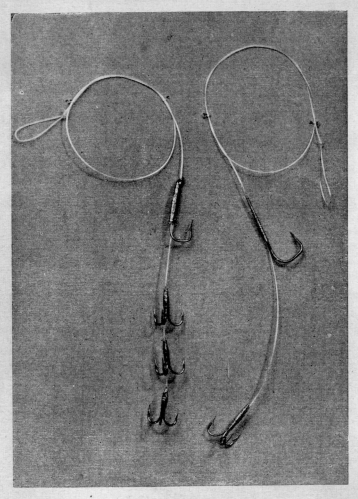

SPINNING FLIGHT, AND LIVE-BAIT FLIGHT, TIED ON STOUT
GUT FOR CLEARER ILLUSTRATION

You see that stream running under the towpath bridge ? Always where a spring enters the main stream small fish will congregate ; you can see bleak rising now. Where bleak and other small fish shoal is always a very likely spot for a good trout to feed. Those are the two important reasons why I am going to fish this water. Another reason is that 10-lb. 2-oz. trout in the case on my wall at home, and the fourth reason is that at this spot two years ago I caught another good fish, a seven-pounder. Of course, I know those two fish are not here to be caught now, but is it fairly certain that one or two good trout are hereabouts."

There was a good fish there, but she was much attached to home, and made no sign of existence during the hour we waited her ; she made a mistake later in the season and graced the dining-table of a friend.

With the evening fast approaching and one more good place to fish, we dropped quietly downstream to Shiplake Hole, seeing nothing move other than a roach or two.

By long casting, the best parts of the river here can be fished from the bank, and here again a considerable stream enters the river under a bridge and the towpath. Bleak, dace and gudgeon always are hereabouts, and several very good trout have been caught by spinning from the bank ; I know of three mounted specimens. On the opposite side of the river the stream is sharper, and often holds a trout, usually of the 5-lb. class.

Having expounded all this to Jack, I set about making the most of the remaining fishing time, spinning a gudgeon with a long cast, but covering also all the unweeded water near the bank.

Beginning about eighty yards above the gate, and having spun down about thirty yards, I ran a fish that I at once knew to be a trout, but not a large one. This was confirmed by the fish leaping twice, revealing himself as a near three-pounder.

A short but strong fight brought him to bank, where he was beached on a sandy patch, unhooked, and allowed to depart to—it was hoped—become a worthwhile specimen.

Spinning down to about a hundred yards below the gate produced one run, which resulted in a pike of between eight and nine pounds being brought to net, and in due course returned to the river.

Examination of the flight disclosed that the gut had been much abraded by the pike's teeth in two places, and as train-time was fast approaching I decided to call it a day, so ordered my crew to scull gently down to the lock, I meanwhile packing up the gear.

In the course of the welcome meal that was brought to table soon after we had reached home, punctual to promise, Jack proclaimed to the family that in all his holidays on the river he had never spent a day that had given him more pleasure, but he remarked, " I wish Uncle had let me bring home that lovely trout."

Thus ended a day that in the essentials of navigation and fishing may justly be termed typical—more or less. The divergence from typical being the beaching of the trout, such an incident does not occur on every outing, far from it, unhappily.

Before turning in the long-expected question was put : " When are you going to have another day ? "

A little gloom was noticed when I replied that I couldn't take another day before Wednesday or Thursday, but most likely would in the interval be able to fish on a few occasions for two or three hours in the early morning. Turning out early was not popular with Jack.

Having promised him that he should accompany me on the chosen day, he retired, sleepy and happy, to a bed from which he turned out in time to be late for breakfast ; he had slept like a dormouse !

Thursday it was that turned out to be our next outing.

CHAPTER VII

A LESS TYPICAL DAY

THE early morning presaged reasonably favourable weather, and again the boy was given choice of venue. His reasoning that we knew there was at least one good trout in those waters made him plump for Shiplake, and our preliminaries before reaching the lock were but a repetition of Saturday's programme.

Before boarding the boat I gave my crew an outline of my intended procedure, which was, instead of going upstream to Sonning and fishing down, to begin at the bottom of the reach and fish up as far as we conveniently could and leave time to scull steadily back to the lock.

The previous season I had seen a five- or six-pound trout in front of the tumbling bay, so a mooring was made about forty yards above the slight stream and in the middle of the lock-cut channel. The depth of overflow here in normal height of the river is small, but little dace and roach love to congregate on the shallow, particularly on sunny days, thus forming an attractive location for a trout.

There being a nice ripple on the water from a gentle westerly breeze was in favour of spinning ; actually there was too little current to carry down a live bait. Careful spinning from our first anchorage, followed by two short

drops downstream, fished blank. I elected to go ashore
and give the weir top a short trial. The sluices were
awkwardly drawn for making a good fishing run, and
the most likely places appeared to be full of pike, of
which I caught three—the biggest between seven and
eight pounds. As two flights were ruined by the teeth
of Esox, I did not linger, and issued instructions to my
navigator to proceed to the corner of the meadow—
actually a large island—where there is a deep hole of
considerable area, which before the present weir was
built was the weir-pool, the " new " weir being much
farther downstream. The only run obtained here was
from a large chub, approximately four pounds, which
was returned unhurt to the river.

Our next move was to the " Danger " pile, to which
the boy moored by means of a length of towline, which
when slackened out a few yards at a time enabled me to
cover all the weir head water that was worth fishing.

Immediately above a drawn sluice or paddles is a
favourite lie for trout ; often a good one or two frequent
the neighbourhood of such a run, and as will be read
before the end of this book is reached, I have had the
pleasure of landing from a really strong head run a heavy
specimen to grace my collection.

On this day nothing so good was to happen, the only
fish seen being a small perch chasing my bait which was
nearly as large as itself. Indicating the spot, I set my
crew to reach the lower end of Phillimore Island, and the
mouth of Borough Marsh opposite. Although a good
trout was known to frequent the mouth of the Marsh,
and a smaller one of about $5\frac{1}{2}$ lb. the vicinity of the black
boathouse alongside the towpath, much spinning was
done over a considerable area without a scale being, so
far as was known, moved.

The next move was to the top of the island, where

according to the bathing boys of the village, and as told to me by two of them who knew a trout from a barbel or a pike, " a great trout often jumps out of the river just there," pointing to a spot about fifteen yards above the point of the island. That was in the previous summer. Let it suffice to record that on this particular day he failed to jump when I was near, neither did he evince any curiosity about my beautiful spinning bait, although I covered patiently every yard of the shallow and the adjacent hole.

There being a favourable breeze, I elected next to fish the bank of Borough Marsh meadow, opposite Shiplake Hole. Having spun down about a hundred yards which covered the best of the water, and yielded not a run from any kind of fish, I wound up, and was with Jack strolling up to the boat when I saw a bleak making a series of long hops at a pace like a sprinter covering the hundred yards in ten seconds dead, from near the middle of the river toward the bank along which we were walking, and not far below where I first began fishing down.

Shortly after there was a swirl and a splash which denoted the demise of that unfortunate bleak.

A bleak does not make long hops at a fast pace just because of his joy of life, but because he is anxious to prolong that life by putting as much distance as possible between himself and a hungry trout. I write trout specifically because a pike does not feed that way, he prefers to dash into a crowd, or wait quietly in cover to engulf a solitary unsuspecting passer-by.

Almost always, if a trout decides to eat a particular fish, he will persist in chasing that fish until it is grabbed, or in the minority of instances, finds cover.

I have noticed, too, that on most occasions a trout works up stream when feeding, so proceeded to make my first stand some thirty to forty yards above where the swirl occurred, spinning gradually down river at about two strides interval, casting across at a slight angle, and working the bait in a sweep to the bank.

It may be instructive to interpolate that in the open reaches I invariably spin fast for trout, but never at the same pace throughout recovery. It is good to vary the rapidity of turning the reel, but not to drop to the slowness that is usual in salmon spinning. Briefly, fast for trout, slow for salmon and pike.

Not many minutes elapsed before there came that thrilling moment when a trout has taken good hold of one's bait, and a few seconds later a " bar of silver " leapt well out of the water, revealing a fish that I could see was between five and six pounds—when put on the scale at home he balanced just over 5½ lb.—and after a strong, lively fight Jack lifted the landing net at exactly the right moment and we were admiring one of Nature's loveliest creations, a beautifully marked and well-fed young trout, an event that called for celebration in the usual manner, and was not allowed to pass unobserved.

Our next move was to the neighbourhood of the spring passing under the towpath, and after fishing and resting the water for about an hour, we were on the point of moving when a number of small fry broke water exactly opposite the mouth of the spring.

Feeling certain that the commotion was not caused by a trout, but realizing the possibility that it might be, I mounted another bait, and after a few casts brought to net a very large perch, but in poor condition, certainly over two pounds in weight and a potential glass caser in December.

Normal lunch time after an early breakfast, and an abnormal appetite induced by the exhilarating Spring morning governed our next move, which was to the spot above the head of St. Patrick's Stream, where we dropped anchor well above the spot where the trout was seen on the preceding Saturday.

Here, with the spinning tackle kept ready for use, a live bait was gradually worked down nearly to the point of the island, and wound up and repeated several times in the course of about a couple of hours ; nothing excited the live bait and no fish showed to the right or to the left of it, but it was spun over and nothing found moving, so on the principle of covering as much water as comfortably possible in the day, we moved up to where in the last bathing season a springboard was fixed, with deep and shallow water adjacent. This water being a favourite haunt of gudgeon, one of that species was mounted as a spinner ; this curious little fish is tougher than a bleak or dace, survives in good order much more casting, and is, in water that is not discoloured, a very killing bait.

This was not one of its killing days, for much patient casting failed to elicit a run, nor was any sign of a trout being near vouchsafed to us.

Next trial was at the barbel hole, where both live bait and spinner were well tried without result, the spinner being snatched away just in time to prevent it from being seized by a pike of about seven pounds, which would probably have meant a ruined flight, and brooding over unkind thoughts, if not words.

From the barbel hole the crew sculled unhurriedly up to Sonning Bridge, Piscator meanwhile keeping a sharp look-out for the sight of a feeding trout, with which his vigilance was not rewarded.

Mooring at the bridge, Jack elected to take a leg-stretcher by walking up to the Lock, whilst I chose to spin to a long way down the towpath, it all being water likely to hold two or three good trout.

Spinning from the stand where on the previous Saturday the small trout had followed my bait, I ran, hooked, and landed what was probably the same fish, which was returned unhurt to the river. Nothing more resulted in the length of the meadow bank, and meeting Jack at the boat, an adjournment to the close-by hotel for tea was made, after which the homeward journey was begun by drifting slowly down stream as far as the head of the St. Patrick's Stream, where I intended to put in at least half an hour, knowing the fish that lived there to be a good one, and well worth catching. I did not catch it that day, nor any other day, but an otter did, and a waterman brought to me its head, and I was not a doubter when told that the trout from which it came was an eight pounder or more.

Deciding to make one last stand at Shiplake Hole, we drifted quietly downstream, keeping a sharp watch for a feeding fish. Arrived at the top end of the Hole, I had the weight lowered in mid-stream, so that the water each side of the boat could be spun over. Two drifts of about twenty-five yards from our first enabled all the best of the water to be fished, which was done without a touch. Packing, sculling down and proceeding to Henley finished a glorious day, typical in practice with our first day, but less typical in the fact that we had a good trout as a reward for our efforts.

I am an elderly man, well beyond three score and ten, and sometimes have difficulty in recalling events that happened only a few years ago, yet can remember vividly all the foregoing incidents and details that occurred over thirty years ago, in 1914.

There are other items also in my memory, such as boiling a clutch of moorhen eggs in an empty meat tin, over a stick fire built between two lumps of concrete ; of seeing the big pike and a smaller companion on the shallow rush-bed—she weighed $17\frac{1}{2}$ lb. in the following November, but I didn't catch her.

Of hearing the cuckoo call for the first time that season, and of the display of Spring flowers in the spinney. I wonder why ? Perhaps it is because of the fact that inside of fifteen months from our memorable days, and when within three days of his twentieth birthday, the erstwhile bright boy, keen student and budding lawyer, became the responsible, although immature, MAN, and died, in France, for his Country, when leading his platoon " over the top," in the War that was to end War.

CHAPTER VIII

OTTERS AND TROUT

THE largest Thames otter I have seen weighed 29 lb. after it had met with a fatal accident near Hurley, but the story thereof is not for these pages.

Otters will eat any kind of fish that comes to mouth, but I believe their first love is an eel. That they will kill and partially devour large trout I have on three occasions seen undeniable evidence.

The largest was certainly in life a twelve or thirteen pounder, the others nine or ten pounders. The chief interest in this note lies in lillustrating the great strength of otters in proportion to their size, for any man accustomed to handling large trout must be aware of the power that such a fish can put into its struggles.

In the upper pool at Hambleden at an early hour in the morning I saw an otter bring ashore a trout of nearly 3 lb. ; my rush to the scene caused the otter to drop its prey and disappear. The trout, being so much injured as to be beyond hope of making recovery, made a toothsome

meal for the lock-keeper and his wife, who—like so
many of my old friends—are no longer alive. This
fact does not, however, suggest that the fish killed them !

A Remarkable Happening

Since writing the foregoing, I have thought that an
incident that occurred to me at New Mills tail water
would be of interest to many readers. In the days
when the above-named mill was working (foreign com-
petition unfortunately compelled its closing down),
there was a very fine back run which also was one of the
finest barbel swims on the Thames. Moored under the
camp-sheathing in this run was a launch which when out
of use was protected by a canvas cover. As usually the
case, this cover had depressions fore and aft the works.
I was spinning this back run for trout, of which the tail
held several, and ran a good fish, which made one complete round of the fast central water and the back run ;
on the second round the fish had reached a point opposite
the launch and leapt high from the water, falling on the
aft depression of the canvas cover. From this the
owner of the launch scooped it with my landing net and
subsequently enjoyed eating a portion of its $7\frac{3}{4}$ lb.
carcase.

Bad Luck—for the Trout !

Between fifty and sixty years ago, on one of the
Royal Regatta days, and close to Henley Bridge, a
7-lb. trout created a great surprise by leaping into a
punt. I saw this fish, which after being photographed,
graced the dining table at a famous hotel near-by.

Some years later, when William Butt was lock-keeper

at Cleeve, near Goring, an eight-pounder leapt in the night into a punt that was moored alongside the island wall.

Butt—who was formerly lock-keeper at Marsh, near Henley, wrote to me an account of this happening, as I had on three or four occasions attempted to catch this worthy specimen, whose actual weight proved my estimate—after I had seen it feeding—to be almost accurate.

During and after publication of the basic matter of the foregoing pages, I received a considerable number of letters, mostly of gratifying character, and some asking questions which I felt could be best dealt with by way of this supplementary chapter.

Loss of Weight of Trout After Capture

Answering three correspondents

Here yet another hoary gibe goes wrong. Contrary to popular fallacy, trout do not invariably gain weight more rapidly after death than they did in life.

In point of fact they lose weight generally in proportion to the care, or want of care, taken in storing them.

By using reasonable care the loss of weight in five or six hours is very small.

The fish should be wrapped carefully—keeping the fins and tail straight—in thin absorbent paper, such as a newspaper, and not on any account in waterproof or greaseproof paper, if it is intended for mounting.

Once so wrapped, the paper should not be frequently removed for exhibition purposes, as stripping of scales may be caused.

If the fish cannot be sent immediately for preservation, store in a cool place out of draught, and under protection from the family cat.

If you can knock up a rough box to take the corpse, good ; if not let the packing be in plenty, and in any case sufficient to keep the fish straight and stiff ; a piece of board, a little longer and wider than the first wrapping will suffice.

Following are a few examples of loss of weight :—

Weighed 9.30 a.m., 8 lb. 5 oz. ; 7.30 p.m., 8 lb. 4 oz.
Weighed 9.0 p.m., 9 lb. 10½ oz. ; 8.0 a.m., 9 lb. 10 oz.
Weighed 8.30 p.m., 9 lb. 1½ oz. ; 8.30 a.m., 8 lb. 14 oz.
Weighed 7.15 p.m., 9 lb. 1 oz. ; 11.45 p.m., 8 lb. 15 oz.
Weighed 11.30 a.m., 10 lb. 5¾ oz. ; 3.0 p.m., 10 lb.
 4 oz.
Weighed 12.0 p.m., 9 lb. 5 oz. ; 9.0 a.m., 9 lb. 2 oz.
Weighed 5.0 p.m., 8 lb. 8 oz. ; 10.0 p.m., 8 lb. 5 oz.
Weighed 2.0 p.m., 10 lb. 2 oz. ; 7.0 p.m., 10 lb.
Weighed 11.0 a.m., 12 lb. 2½ oz. ; 5.0 p.m., 11 lb.
 15 oz.
Weighed 12.0 a.m., 10 lb. 6 oz. ; 8.0 p.m., 10 lb. 3 oz.

Some of the above spent a few hours wrapped in paper or cloth in a punt in warm weather.

Careless keeping would cause loss of weight double or more the above-named amounts.

THE THAMES FLIGHT

Answering six correspondents

In my early angling days spinning the open water was much more in vogue than now, although the reels available—even the best—were far below the present-day standard of excellence.

There was little casting from the reel, that method being in its infancy, and nearly all spinning was done by hand by allowing the recovered line to coil on the floor of the punt or on the bank ; an alternative used by more accomplished spinners was to coil the line on the extended left palm as it was recovered, and another method when spinning fast water was to gather the line in figure of eight fashion in the left hand.

Drawbacks and disasters there were, particularly to the clumsy people who sometimes moved a foot in the punt and stepped on and cut the line, or to others who failed to watch the fall of the line on the bank and fouled twigs or grass heads.

Coiling on the palm of the left hand was pretty work and called for a good deal of care, especially when a trout was run as the loops depended eighteen inches or so from the hand.

Figure of eight was practised by only a small proportion of spinners, and called for considerable skill in both hooking and playing a fish.

The foregoing methods were capable of producing, and in the hands of a practised spinner, did produce, very attractive movements from a bleak, dace or gudgeon spun by a Thames flight, and I frequently revert to the old style, but the coming of the centre-pin reel gradually wiped out Thames style spinning, and very few anglers now use it.

The Thames flight, however, stood its ground with the regular " old hand " trout fishers—of whom only a very small number remain—who would have none of the artificial fish and other variations of bait which began to come in shoals to the tackle shops.

My first flights were brought from a Henley tackle dealer long since dead, and I soon discovered that they did not wear well ; the varnish, which was laid over and not soaked through the silk, chipped and exposed the whippings—which probably were piece-work tied—and soon came to the stage of needing re-tying. As I did this job of work myself it seemed logical to begin at the beginning and tie the tackle properly, so with few exceptions I have tied all my spinning flights nearly the whole of my fishing life.

The lip-hooks, procurable over a long term of years, were of four patterns as shown by rough sketches A, B, C and D.

A, B and C are heavily drawn and enlarged to ensure clearer reproduction.

All served their purpose of making the flight adjustable to various lengths and to close the mouth of bait, but if called upon to hook a trout all were equally bad.

Pattern A had gut loops whipped to the shank, and when these loops became soaked they ceased to function properly, and quickly wore rough and thin as well as allowing the hook to slip.

Pattern B with its right-angled projecting steel eyes, often cut the gut, and gave short service to every flight.

Patterns C and D, with oblique steel eyes, were better, but still unsatisfactory.

Hooks such as these are current to-day and are used largely for certain types of tackle quite successfully.

It happened fifty years or so ago when I was out with Bob Young, that we fell in at Hurley with an excellent professional fisherman of Maidenhead, one of the well-known Andrews family and an old friend of Bob's, who, with a client, was fishing the river for trout from Maidenhead to Hambleden and back.

Andrews and his client were complaining forcibly that they had that morning lost a brace of good trout, both through defects of the gut-looped lip-hook, type A

Andrews remarked, " I wish we could do without the long dash loops, and I have an idea we can by making the lip-hook to slide ; anyhow I am going to try."

On his way down from Hambleden Andrews called on

Young at Medmenham Ferry and showed him a roughly-tied sample of his idea, which Bob was quick to see was good.

Between them they elaborated the idea, and Andrews stripped the gut eyes from a hook of pattern A, the shank of which he then wrapped with fine silk. The hook was then laid to the gut and the two surrounded by a piece of quill from the pen-feather of a small bird, whipped neatly over with silk and varnished.

Properly tied the lip-hook slides evenly but firmly to adjustment when the gut is soaked, and the link of the flight has a straight pull instead of two or three twists.

For many years I used this type of lip-hook, until I lost the large trout referred to in a former chapter of this book.

After making a number of experiments I arrived at the conclusion that Kendal Sneck such as figures E.3 and F.4 was the hook to supplant all former types, and from about the time of losing the twelve-pounder to the present-day I have used none other.

The tying is done as above described, the gut being first passed through the eye, which effectively prevents any chance of the hook being drawn from its sheath, an incident that sometimes—but rarely—happened to the original type, and only then when not perfectly tied.

For flights for small-bait, No. 3 should be used, for bleak and small dace, No. 4, and for larger bait, No. 5.

The spacing and size of the three triples also should be varied to suit different lengths of bait.

FLIES

Answering two letters

As I found that I met with consistent success with " sombre " flies, which somewhat resembled fry when worked, I made no experiments with " gaudy " flies, but know no reason why they should not be effective if fished wet and worked with movements to imitate little fish.

GENERALLY

I wish to express to all my correspondents my thanks for their letters, and am naturally very pleased to know that my series of articles has been so well received by my Thames Brethren of the Angle.

CHAPTER IX

MORE ABOUT TACKLE

THE spinning flight illustrated is the middle of three sizes which I usually use, and is actual size, the gut excepted, which is medium salmon, the flight being one of a set tied for fishing the Avon, where the salmon run to an average of twenty pounds. In baiting it an important point is to handle tenderly the small fish that you hope is going to attract a trout.

It must, of course, be killed, and to effect this with the least damage I sever with a small bradawl the backbone at the base of the head. Insert one hook of the last triple lightly through the skin at the fork of the tail, the second hook must be adjusted to deflect the tail to an angle of 45° and inserted in the side of the bait, after carefully judging its exact position.

The bait's tail must not be set square, neither must it be at too slight an angle ; in the former case it will spin in very ugly shape, and in the second it will revolve " once a week," if at all.

The action aimed at is a clean, straight, unwobbly revolution.

Having set the middle triple, keep the bait perfectly straight and insert in the lateral line one hook of the third triple.

Still keeping the bait straight, adjust the lip-hook and insert it through both lips of the bait ; if a bleak or dace, upward through the lower lip ; if a gudgeon, downward through the upper lip ; this may seem a trivial detail, but it is important, and means just the difference between the bait spinning, or slithering through the water in the best way to attract pike, which at this time of year one does not willingly invite.

The live-bait tackle shown is the largest pattern, and actual size ; I prefer to have three or four sizes with a fixed lip-hook rather than one that is adjustable, for the reason that often a trout is hooked on only the single hook ; if this slipped an inch on the trout taking the bait the probable result would be a pricked and enlightened fish.

For the small extra cost per dozen always use the best quality hooks that money can buy ; a poorly-tempered and ill-shaped hook is dear as a gift, and may lead to much disappointment.

The gut, too, should be the best procurable, and for obstructed weirs and heavy streams need not be finer than 9/5 or medium, whilst fine, and sometimes extra fine, may safely be used in open reaches and quiet, un-obstructed pools ; this, of course, depends upon the build of rod, and the man behind it ; all should be in unison and handled in a workmanlike way.

In any case it is inadvisable to fish very fine until you have experienced what a good trout can do in the way of gymnastics and running ; here in particular I am addressing the new hand at Thames trouting.

CHAPTER X

ABOUT A TEN-POUNDER

IN *A Fisherman's Angles* that charming scribe, Patrick Chalmers, tells of a ten-pound trout that was caught on the regatta course at Henley, and he devotes to it a chapter called " Up in the Morning Early."

A quotation from the chapter is not without interest and a touch of humour.

" And as for trout, it was not a case of getting up early, but of not going to bed at all. In those days I was serving my apprenticeship to Father Thames, Father Thames and his Trout, and no trouble was too great for me. So when a boatman at Marlow told me that a ten-pound trout fed at three a.m. below the Point, and that dawn by dawn he saw it when he visited the eel baskets, I could not rest for thinking of the great fellow.

" I lived in London, and it seemed simple to take the theatre train from Paddington and be by the misty river at one o'clock in the June morning. And as day came a-tip-toe over Quarry Woods, a school of bleak sprung splashing and dashing. For the shadow of Death was among them—the big trout breakfasted.

"And my third throw caught him. It seems a pity to have to say that his weight was five and a half pounds, and *not* the ten that had tempted me. But he was as pretty as a picture, thick and short and shapely, and when I took the milk train to town, where I must be at my desk by nine o'clock, I felt that I had had my return ticket's worth.

"But here is one of the few early morning trout that *did* weigh ten pounds—even a little more than ten.

"In a summer gloaming the —— Thames Angler ——(modesty impels me to substitute dashes for words —A. E. H.) leant upon Henley Bridge and talked trout to a professional fisherman. (Known locally as the Duke of Teck!—A. E. H.) Down the Regatta Course, of a sudden, a near-pound roach imitated a flying-fish, imitated it all across the river.

"'A big trout,' said the professional.

"'Yes,' agreed the amateur, and the pair went their thoughtful and respective ways.

"At two a.m. the angler looked out of his window into a lovely quietness of water, green elms and beeches, and a June day just commencing.

"The church clock struck the half after two.

"As it struck six, the professional, crossing the bridge, looked down and saw the amateur busy about his boat.

"Jocosely he called : 'Going out after him ? '

"'Not much good now,' returned the other.

"'How's that, sir ? '

"'Because I have him in the punt-well,' said the —— Thames Angler ——."

This fish lived in deep water near the finish of the

Regatta Course, and was rarely seen, even by workmen engaged all day on neighbouring buildings.

I had seen him a few times—when not fishing—and it transpired that the professional also had seen him a number of times in the very early morning, on not entirely lawful occasions, intimately connected with eels ! That was why we agreed when we saw him from Henley Bridge.

The morning of this trout's downfall was very quiet and calm, the surface of the clear water like a plate of glass, so obviously spinning was not likely to have better effect than to scare the fish.

A large live gudgeon was the bait used, which the trout took deeply with a vicious pull, and short, powerful run.

He made no long runs, and fought stubbornly like a pike, once getting dangerously near the light mooring line near which the angler stood, prepared, if necessary, to cut.

Trouble avoided, the fine gear stood up to its work, and in about a quarter of an hour the landing net came into use with the happy result, for the angler, recorded above.

CHAPTER XI

GROWTH AND LONGEVITY OF TROUT

SIXTEEN or more years ago, when fishing at Mapledurham on a very warm day, I felt the need of a cool drink and walked about eighty yards to the lock cottage to have a soda squash, there being nothing with a kick in it to be had nearer than a mile away.

Before leaving for the lock, I leant my rod over the weir beam, facing upstream ; on the tackle was a small live bait which I adjusted so that the little fish just broke the surface of the water, thinking that thus it would be safe and unlikely to attract a trout.

On my return a few minutes later the bait was missing. With the idea that it might have been taken by a killable fish, I mounted another bait and fished it across the front of the weir. It was taken almost immediately by a small trout that measured 15½ inches. I marked it by fixing to its adipose fin a silver wire staple with flat top, on which was impressed the letter H. The fish returned to the water strong and well, and at the same spot. A year later it was again caught by my friend Patrick Chalmers when it measured 19½ inches ; he, knowing the circumstance of its marking, and being much interested, returned the trout fit and well in the same place.

Two seasons later, when fishing in company with Patrick, I again caught the fish, which, weighed on an accurate spring balance to which was fitted a fine waterproof net cradle, just over 5 lb.

This time the trout was returned to the river below the weir, and in *A Fisherman's Angles*, by Patrick Chalmers, the author refers to the incident in these words :

" But if you catch a little trout, or a big trout, it is never too late to give him his life, and, only last season, I saw five pounds of gold dust and silver go back to become ten pounds—bread upon the waters indeed ! "

I have not fished at Mapledurham for about eight years, nor have I heard of the marked trout being again caught.

Scale reading has proved that trout on the Thames will grow to a weight of 9 lb. 10½ oz. in six years, and such a fish if not killed might easily reach fourteen or fifteen pounds.

To write definitely as to the length of life of trout in such a big water as the Thames would be foolish and unprovable, but that some specimens have a long span of life I am certain, twenty or more years in favourable conditions, such as deep and quiet waters, and the proximity of a good food supply.

One can be perfectly satisfied as to the identity of a particular trout in a particular corner without being able to provide lawyer's proof of identity ; and the late Robert Young of Medmenham and I knew of two such fish for over twenty years, both were very large and I tried many times to catch them, but never had a pull from either. Big fish such as these will feed on half-pound roach and large dace, and show themselves irregularly and infrequently, whereas a smaller fish in collecting a dozen or more bleak will show many times, and in favourable conditions almost daily for some weeks of the season.

For eight years at least—and, I believe, nine—some friends and I made a kind of pet of a trout that we estimated would weigh nearly six pounds. He or she—for convenience we will say he—was unmistakable, for he had a wall eye. He appeared suddenly one season and took up his position at the outflow corner of a mill thorough, where he could be seen daily for many weeks of the season. His staple dish seemed to be minnows, which abounded in those days, and we never saw him chasing bleak. Late in the season he disappeared, probably into the deepest part of the mill-tail, but reappeared regularly each season when the warm days of April came round, until his final disappearance in the eighth or ninth year, which we always thought was hastened by an otter, there being a family of these interesting creatures in residence on an adjacent island. We never tried to catch him, and the miller would never allow any other angler to fish the pool in the trout season. My point in writing so fully of this trout is the fact that in all the years of our acquaintance he appeared never to grow an inch, and in the last year or two became much thinner ; also in a particular light one could plainly see his big old head with its parrot-like jaws, which seemed to indicate that he was an aged fish when first he adopted the corner as his permanent quarters. He may, of course, have died of old age ; or grown so weak that he became easy prey for one of the otter family.

In all probability that trout was at least fifteen years old when he died.

CHAPTER XII

ABOUT YOUR SPECIMEN TROUT

HAVING caught your specimen, and having had him —or what is more likely, her—artistically mounted in a bow-fronted glass case, take care of him. Do not display him in a very warm spot, nor hang him on a damp wall. The former may cause the back of the case to crack, and the latter will cause the paper strapping of the case to open and peel. Satisfy yourself occasionally that the case is sound, and if one day you find that a fracture of either wood or paper has occurred, take steps at once to remedy the defects.

Having done this, bore a tiny hole in the back of the case only sufficiently large to allow the needle of a hypodermic syringe to easily pass, then inject an insecticide spray of formalin, which will be supplied in suitable solution by your chemist ; neatly plug the hole with a piece of match-stick and cover the area with a piece of gummed paper about an inch square. If necessary, at any time, to repeat the operation, push the small piece of match through, replug and cover as before.

If the crack in the back has occurred in a suitable place, the spray can be introduced before repairing the defect.

I have known several good specimens ruined through their owner neglecting to take elementary precautions to keep them in perfect condition. A well-preserved specimen fish is far better than a mediocre picture.

CHAPTER XIII

HOW TO COOK YOUR TROUT

AGAIN—having killed your trout, and found her not up to the weight that you long ago decided should be the minimum of her kind in your collection, the next business is to consider closely the disposal of the body. This may well be a ponderous business, calling for much thought and some manipulation.

First of all you think—I have not tasted trout for so many months, it may be years, but in either event you may need all the fingers and thumbs of both hands to provide the answer. However, you over-ride the selfish thought, and begin to recall that A.B. gave me a brace of birds and a hare last winter ; C.D. sent to me at Christmas a fine hen turkey ; then, of course, I cannot forget that E.F. sent a couple of brace of grouse sixteen months ago ; and so on. You realize, also, that on the whole your trout is financially about the equal of either of your friends' presents, but, alas ! you cannot send it to more than one, and to cut such a fish would be little less than vandalism ; overmore, what is one small fish among so many, even in these days of austerity queues, points and what-not ? You begin to see daylight, and resolve that the first thing to do is to decide whether to keep the trout yourself, or to give it away " in a present." The best way to find the answer is the old-fashioned one, of tossing a coin, the operation that has decided things of far greater moment in the past, and will again until the end of time. The formula will be " Heads I keep it ; tails I give it away "—that is the usual, even constant formula. In the absence of a sovereign, a penny will do, and in the interest of honesty the coin must have a head one side and a tail the other ; such things as two-headed pennies do exist—but that of course is by the way, it wouldn't really occur to you. Up goes the coin, spinning like a phantom, down it comes, flat plop, and tail up ! You mentally say you didn't mean a " sudden death " toss to be decisive, but " two out of three " ! So up goes the coin again, down it comes, head up : as you were ! For the third and last time up goes, and down comes, the penny, landing, to your unexpressed satisfaction, head up, so you keep the body.

In these days of scanty service, and the growth of personal utility, it will probably fall to the angler's lot to " clean " the fish. This should be done with much care, and with little water ; always clean a trout and a salmon as dry as possible ; in fact in most essentials your trout is a salmon, and it should be cooked in the same way as a salmon, but we must finish cleaning her first. Scrape very lightly to remove any loose scales,

F

cut off tail and fins, remove gills ; and now with care
to avoid bursting the gall bladder, which may ruin your
fish, take out the traill, and with the end of a blunt knife
scrape away the " blood "—that is not blood—from the
backbone. The " traill " will include the liver, the roe,
which will be small, and other innards, probably some
bleak or gudgeon. All this, the gills excepted, can be
boiled separately, and will make a much appreciated meal
or meals, for " Nigger " and " Jean."

Having finished the cleaning, rub inside and outside
with cooking salt, and hang up to drain until fish-kettle
time.

In my opinion, boiling is the one and only way to cook
a trout of 4 lbs. and upward. This may be done with the
fish entire, or cut into steaks about $1\frac{1}{2}$ inches thick. By
the latter way the fish is more evenly cooked, also it is
more easily and neatly served.

Whether whole or in steaks, put the fish into boiling
water, in which is a heaped tablespoonful of salt, also a
level spoonful of vinegar. According to the weight of
the fish, boil for half an hour and upward, until by test
the flesh will easily leave the backbone.

Serve very hot, and if you or your guests—there will
be guests because it is an occasion—like your fish sauced,
there are many sauces to suit most tastes, ranging from
plain vinegar or lemon juice up to the well-known
Hollandaise. In the days of plenty, melted butter and
minced parsley was sometimes served, the parsely when
heated with the butter being sufficiently cooked.

Personally, I prefer the untampered flavour of the
fish, and add only a little of the liquor in which the
fish was boiled, or a spoonful of plain melted butter,
when obtainable.

Naturally, these large trout vary in quality, and a fat
well-grown hen fish is, in my opinion, the equal of most

salmon, and better than some ; its flesh will probably be pink and creamy, altogether delectable ; whilst an old fish will cut yellowish-white and be lacking in curd and flavour.   In either case, it will probably taste better to its captor than to any other partaker.

CHAPTER XIV

HOW TO CAMOUFLAGE A ROD

THE glint of sunlight on a highly-finished rod is annoying to many anglers, and may be scaring to trout, and I have often been asked how best to destroy the flash. A very simple way to deaden the brilliance of coach, copal, or other bright varnish is to clean off with American turpentine and a piece of soft rag all grease from the rod.   This will not injure the protective varnish, which should then be given a coat of " egg-shell " or " flat " varnish ; this normally can be obtained from most colour-men or decorators.

It is very quickly applied and dry, and all danger of abrasion, and of exposing the cement at the apex of the hexagonal joints, also of roughening the silk whippings is avoided—this being very likely to occur unless great care be used in dulling the whippings and cane with pumice powder, which is sometimes advocated.

The treatment is equally good for built, solid wood, or hollow cane rods. A further advantage is that the weather-resisting qualities of the body varnish are unimpaired.

If one does not object to the grain of the wood or cane, or to the whipping being obliterated, the rod can

be freed from grease and given a coat of green " flat "
paint, light, medium or dark, to choice ; this paint is
commonly obtainable from colourmen, who will make it
specially to shade. Here, again, the protection given to
the rod by the body varnish is not reduced.

CHAPTER XV

MORE ABOUT SPINNING

ALWAYS I have known that the distance travelled
by a line in the course of a few hours' spinning
must be great, but until March of this year (1946) never
felt sufficiently interested in the subject to work out an
analysis.

It became a duty to do so when I accepted an invita-
tion to test thoroughly and report upon a new nylon-
plaited spinning line.

The figures were so impressive that I feel sure that it
will be of considerable interest to include in this volume
a—

REPORT OF TEST

*made by A. Edward Hobbs on a nylon line
manufactured by Messrs. British Nylon
Spinners Ltd., 72, Lockhurst Lane, Coventry.*

The line was originally 100 yards in length, and of a
breaking strain of 14 lb.

It was used in conjunction with a 9 ft. 6 in. greenheart

spinning rod fitted with porcelain rings, and a 4-in. " Aerial " reel.

The baits used were 2-in., 2½-in. and 3-in. Devons, and Sprat Devons, and a Geen's spinning lead with each.

The river on which the test was made was the Hampshire Avon, on pools of mainly moderately fast water.

The particulars which follow are the result of seven days' fishing, and are tabulated after close checking by a reliable time-piece, and a tape measure.

After 3½ days' use a length of 5 feet was cut from the fore end of the line, and shall be called Sample No. 1.

After a further 3½ days' fishing, another length of 5 feet was cut from the line, and shall be called Sample No. 2.

In the course of the first 3½ days' fishing the number of casts made in 20 minutes was closely checked, such check being repeated on two other occasions on each day.

The distance cast also was checked by standard measure.

The number of casts made in the first 3½ days was over 1,000, but for the purpose of this report the figure of 1,000 is adopted.

The average length of each cast was over 25 yards, but for the purpose of this report the figure of 25 yards is adopted.

Therefore the line travelled through the rings 25,000 yards—14 miles and 360 yards—in making the forward cast.

Obviously it travelled the same distance in being recovered—a total of 28 miles 720 yards.

In recovering the line the resistance—or friction—imposed by the strength of stream, pull and weight of bait, and spinning lead was very much greater than the comparative absence of friction in projecting the line, to which the greatest strain (and friction) was applied in the fore-end of 5 feet, called No. 1 Sample, when starting the cast.

The friction of recovery was added to by occasional hitching of the bait in weed and other obstructive objects ; once in each $3\frac{1}{2}$ days heavy strain being required to free the bait when exceptionally fast.

The second $3\frac{1}{2}$ days were occupied almost precisely as the first $3\frac{1}{2}$ days, and the same figures apply ; therefore the line travelled in all 56 miles 1,400 yards in 7 days' use.

Under test at the Retail Trading Standards Association laboratory in Henley-on-Thames, No. 1 Sample broke at a stress of between $13\frac{1}{2}$ and 14 lb., the sample undergoing four breaking strains.

No. 2 Sample yielded almost identical results, and in both samples particular care was observed in testing the forward *two feet*, the point at which friction with the top ring of the rod was greatest.

Throughout the seven days the line fished admirably and as sweetly as any dressed line that I have used in over sixty years, with the advantage that, being minus any dressing, it is finer than a dressed line of equal breaking strain.

BLEAK, MOUNTED ON THAMES FLIGHT.

Should be spun to fish about eighteen inches below the surface, in other than shallow water.

It will be found necessary to vary the weight of trace lead according to the pace of the stream and the size of bait, but this detail must be decided by the observation of the angler on the spot, as a definite statement here might be misleading.

There are several patterns of quickly changeable leads obtainable at most tackle-dealers.

To mount a live-bait, insert the single hook carefully up and through centrally both lips of a bleak or dace, and down through the top lip only of a gudgeon.

In both cases insert one hook of the triple through a tiny piece of the skin near the front of the dorsal fin, taking care to leave the gut between the hooks slightly slack, otherwise the bait will tend to sway and wobble, and swim unnaturally.

CHAPTER XVI

"MY MOST EXCITING CATCH"

'TWAS a bleak day in the first week of June, the sort of day on which bleak are very hard to come by; east wind, strong and thin, cloudy sky, rough water, and temperature that made a sweater very welcome wear even when taking the exercise demanded by a spell of bank-spinning.

The ever-reliable Bob Young—now over the Styx—with punt and gear meticulously ship-shape awaited me at the appointed time at Medmenham Ferry, and he, like myself, was disgruntled by the unpropitious weather for trout-fishing.

We exchanged our views about the elements in words perhaps more incisive than refined, then came down to the question of the moment : What shall we do, where shall we go ?

A rising barometer indicated that the east wind was likely to persist, and we knew that the only water to fish with a certain amount of comfort was Hambleden Weir, with its four pools and three beautiful tumbling bays.

In deference to Bob's oft-expressed theory, " they must feed sometimes no matter what the weather is like," I spun over a number of likely spots on the way up, the only result being the capture of a 3-lb. jack— called by Bob a " scriper "—and the spoiling of a perfect gut flight by the teeth of the said scriper—an incident that led to more unrefined speech.

As anticipated, we found Hambleden pools nicely sheltered from the piercing wind, and from the punt manœuvred in Bob's masterly manner I cast out and retrieved several hundreds of yards of spinning line without attracting a run from even a scriper.

An interval for lunch and a smoke rested the water for an hour, then from the platforms and steps I tried every likely corner and run without touching a fish of any description.

With Bob's expressed opinion—" This is a bad egg, sir "—I did not disagree, and suggested shoving back to the Ferry to put in an hour or so spinning over the deep ballast-holes which are numerous about there, always likely to hold a trout, and from which we had in recent seasons bagged several good fish.

Again nothing doing, so I asked to be taken down to Hurley Weir—from which we had permission to fish at any time—where the wind would blow across and be somewhat broken by the big trees : a much better proposition than persisting in fishing the open water with a miniature sea running.

Arrived at the Weir, my watch indicated that the hour was past when the portals of a licensed house should be in appealing position, so suggested to Bob—who recently had made good from a bout of 'flu—that he should take the punt across to the tow-path, walk down to " The Bell " and have a good warm up with the appropriate medicine—Scotch *was* Scotch in those days, and only 3s. 6d. a bottle !

" Leave the landing-net, hitcher, and a couple of gudgeon, Bob, I may want one or all before you come back." Twigs in the piles often called for the hitcher's help, and on a number of occasions the landing-net had been in commission.

My last words were—" Don't hurry back, Bob, I shall manage all right." Bob met an old gamekeeper friend from Marlow and didn't hurry ; it took them two and a half hours to celebrate the occasion !

The weir was running very awkwardly, one big iron sluice being drawn, which pulled down the head-water so that only a dribble was flowing over the tumbling bays, leaving a comparatively small area of fishable water, which was well and carefully covered within an hour and a half, the only result being a dash at the spinning gudgeon by a small trout, which partly detached the bait from the flight, fortunately without hooking itself.

Earlier in the season Bob had seen a good trout feeding above the weir, and on two occasions I had tried for it, catching, on the second occasion, a 12-lb. pike. Pulling Bob's leg when the fish was on the punt floor, I said, " You are a fine sort of fisherman, not knowing the difference between a pike and a trout."

His reply, " I am certain it was a trout I saw here, and a good one, too," I knew perfectly well to be truthful, for if Bob said he had seen a trout, and that it was an eight, nine or ten-pounder, I could be confident it was that sort of fish and that sort of weight.

Weary of fishing the unfavourable lower water and there being still a heavy ripple from the strong breeze, I decided to spin above the weir.

At the most it meant only half a dozen or so casts from the cobbler across the stream to cover in a likely way all the fishable water, and at the same time to keep the bait properly spinning.

In my second cast, just as the bait was nearing the edge of the strong straight draw down to the open sluice came that delightful thrill of a heavy fish making a determined grab at its objective and getting well hooked.

Two or three seconds of " stay put " on the bottom, my rod bent to a half circle and a strong stress on my tackle, then off like a rocket down through the sluice went the fish, my fingers on the drum of the winch burning with the friction of putting on as much strain as I estimated my " medium " gut would stand.

I never have less than 150 yards—including backing— of line on my winch, and on several occasions, of which this was one, have had the greater part of 100 yards run out by a big trout.

This fish never surfaced, and either stopped at the end of its long run or worked round in the current, I did not bother to ascertain which, as I felt confident it must be firmly hooked after so violent a " take." I drew about 20 yards of line off the winch and allowed it to follow the weir run, put my rod safely braced in the trolley rail, ran along to collect the hitcher, hooked up and cut the line—beautifully dressed, and 10s. 6d. per 100 yards those days—on the down-stream side, knotted it to the winch line, wound up the long slack, and found, to my great joy, that the trout was still on and moving, having missed the one far-away obstruction that I feared might be fouled had it borne to the right. After eight or nine more minutes I realized that the end of the exciting fight was nearing, and always before it had been a two-handed job landing a good fish at this weir; but Bob was far away and not another being could reach me had there been one in sight, there being a locked gate on my left and no craft on my right.

I edged cautiously towards the landing-net, but not cautiously enough, for I sat down very hard on the slippery weedy concrete, getting extremely wet and soiled at the base of impact.

Fortunately I kept my rod up and line taut, so no damage was done, and the trout, after two more good runs, was guided safely over the landing-net, and fish and net put through the rails on to the weir island, where the knock-out was administered.

I had just finished washing the fish, wrapping it in a newspaper, and putting another bait on my flight when Bob arrived. " Seen anything, sir?" " Yes, Bob, I've got one for the pot on the plank on the island."

Bob's pleasure when he saw the big and beautiful fish was equalled only by his great disappointment at having missed all the fun. This disappointment I did my best a little later to appease at The Ferry Hotel (no longer extant), Medmenham, and I, too, found a couple of bracers not unwelcome.

The inscription on the glass case reads : " Thames Trout, weight 9 lb. 5 oz. Caught by A. E. Hobbs, June, 1897."

From the foregoing a moral may be deduced : No day is ever " completely hopeless " for catching fish, and the line longest in the water if properly fished is most likely to be successful.

I am sometimes asked why I have so many trout set up and my answer is always the same : " I love to sit and catch them over again."

INDEX

Coarse Fish

By E. MARSHALL-HARDY   *Illustrated.* 7s. 6d. *net*

The Field : " Much information which is not readily available elsewhere. . . Altogether, this is a most enjoyable and useful book which no angler interested in coarse fish will regret buying."

Tackle-Making for Anglers

By L. VERNON BATES   *Illustrated.* 10s. 6d. *net*

Scottish Field : " All that the amateur need ever know about tackle-making at home. Almost the first and certainly the best thing of its kind."

Fly-Tying : Principles and Practice

By MAJ. SIR GERALD BURRARD   *Illustrated.* 8s. 6d. *net*

Shooting Times : " A complete guide to the principles and practice of fly-tying." *New and Revised Edition.*

Angling for Brown Trout

By A. R. Harris Cass   *Illustrated in line and half-tone.*
8s. 6d. net

This excellent little book has been written with the object of assisting the unsuccessful or only moderately successful anglers for trout. It is not too much to say that if the advice which the author gives is fully utilized there will be many fewer creels.

Threadline ABC

By Alexander Wanless   *Illustrated. 2s. 6d. net*

In order that the angler may be able to refer instantly to any point about which he is in doubt, the book is presented in alphabetical form. It embodies the twenty-five years of the writer's experience of intensive thread-line angling.

Angling Diversions

By A. Courtney Williams   *Illustrated in line and half-tone 8s. 6d. net*

This book can justly be described as a " different kind " of fishing book, and one which is bound to interest and delight anglers of all ages, whether they be expert or not. Within its pages will be found a fascinating story of fish and fishing from the time of the Romans to that of King Edward VII.